PC maintenance

Preparing for A+ Certification

Workbook

Faithe Wempen

EMCParadigm

Developmental Editor	Michael Sander
Cover Designer	Jennifer Wreisner, Leslie Anderson
Text Designer	Leslie Anderson
Desktop Production	Leslie Anderson, Erica Tava
Copyeditor	Joy McComb

Publishing Team: George Provol, Publisher; Janice Johnson, Director of Product Development; Tony Galvin, Acquisitions Editor; Lori Landwer, Marketing Manager; Shelley Clubb, Electronic Design and Production Manager.

Text ISBN 0-7638-1908-5
Product Number 03596

© 2004 by Paradigm Publishing Inc.
Published by **EMC**Paradigm
875 Montreal Way
St. Paul, MN 55102

(800) 535-6865
E-mail: educate@emcp.com
Web Site: www.emcp.com

Printed in the United States of America
10 9 8 7 6 5 4 3 2

CONTENTS

PART 1
Personal Computer Basics

In this first section of the workbook, you will demonstrate your understanding and mastery of some basic computer skills. By completing the worksheets in this section, you will demonstrate your competence in the following areas:

- Identifying the parts of desktop and notebook PCs
- Working with handheld computers such as PDAs
- Converting between various numbering system such as binary, decimal, and hexadecimal
- Setting up an environment for working on PCs that minimizes the risk of ESD damage
- Protecting yourself from electrical and other hazards when working inside a PC
- Cleaning PCs, monitors, keyboards, and input devices such as mice and trackballs
- Cleaning printers
- Identifying and implementing proper disposal methods for hazardous materials
- Determining the minimum power supply wattage needed for a PC
- Removing and installing PC power supplies
- Installing and testing a UPS
- Using a multimeter to measure voltage

These skills are important to master because they will keep you—and the equipment— safe as you venture into other topics later in the book. For example, knowing how to prevent equipment from being damaged by ESD can help you avoid ruining a costly motherboard when you are removing it from or installing it into a PC case. And understanding how capacitors store an electrical charge even after the device is unplugged can help you avoid getting shocked.

1 Computing Overview

Skill-building toward a career as a PC technician begins with a solid basic understanding of computer hardware. Students with little or no prior experience with computer hardware will want to start with this first set of projects, designed to build familiarity and comfort with the internal and external components that comprise a typical computer system.

Project 1A: Identifying the Parts of a PC

Time to Complete: 20 minutes

Needed: A typical PC; Web access (optional)

Safety: Make sure the PC is turned off and unplugged; do not touch any of the internal parts unnecessarily

Reference: Pages 6 through 19 of the textbook

1. Label the parts on the following photos.

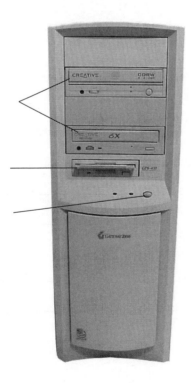 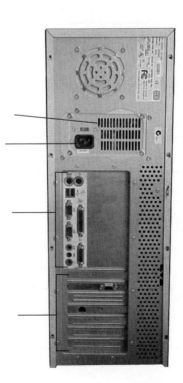

2. Unplug any cables on the back of your own PC. Make notes about where each is connected, so that you can reconnect them later. Then, with all connecting cables removed from your PC, draw a diagram of the front and back, and label the parts on your diagram.

3. How many buttons are there on the front of your PC, and what are their purposes?

_____

_____

_____

4. How many LEDs are on the front of your PC, and what are their purposes?

_____

_____

_____

5. On the following photo, circle the screws that you would need to remove in order to take the cover off the PC.

6. Remove the cover from your PC, and describe below how you did it. How many screws did you remove, if any? What type of screwdriver did you use? Did the entire cover come off or only a side panel?

_____

_____

7. Label the internal parts of the PC on the following photo.

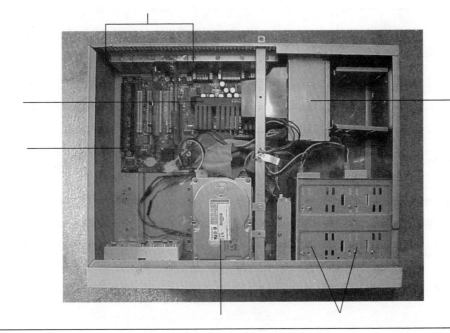

8. Draw a diagram of the inside of your own PC, and label as many parts as you can identify.

9. How many power supply connectors are free inside your PC?

    _____

10. List the drives that are installed on your PC.

    _____

    _____

11. How many expansion boards are installed in the motherboard?

    _____

12. Replace the cover on your PC, including replacing any screws you removed. If you discover any hints or tricks for working with your particular PC case, note them here.

    _____

    _____

    _____

13. Reconnect the cables you disconnected from the back of your PC, and start it up to make sure it still works.

14. On the Web, find as much information as you can about this PC, such as CPU speed and type, motherboard type, amount of RAM installed, and any other data that is available. You might use the PC's model number, manufacturer name, and/or serial number as the basis for your search. List the URL at which you found the information.

    http://_____

Project 1B: Identifying the Parts of a Notebook PC

Time to Complete: 5 to 10 minutes
Needed: A notebook PC
Reference: Pages 19 through 20 of the textbook

1. Label the parts of the notebook computer shown below.

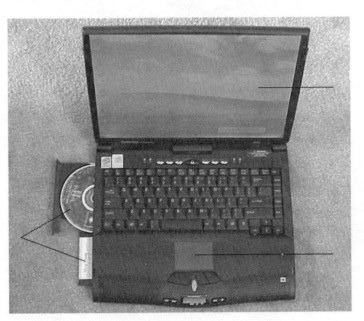

Side

2. On the keyboard below, write in the letters of the following keys to show where they are located on your notebook PC.

a. Ctrl

b. Alt

c. Fn

d. Windows key (⊞)

e. Page Up

f. Page Down

g. Home

h. End

i. Insert

j. Delete

k. Scroll Lock

l. Pause

m. Break

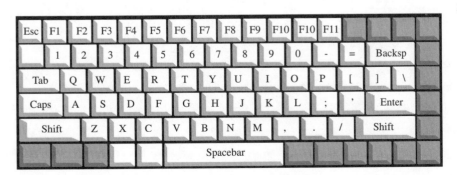

3. What type of pointing device does your notebook PC have?

    _____

4. Match the following uses to the connectors shown.

    a. External monitor
    b. External keyboard or mouse
    c. Printer
    d. Phone cable (modem)
    e. Ethernet network

    f. Docking station
    g. Legacy serial (COM) port
    h. PC Card
    i. External speakers

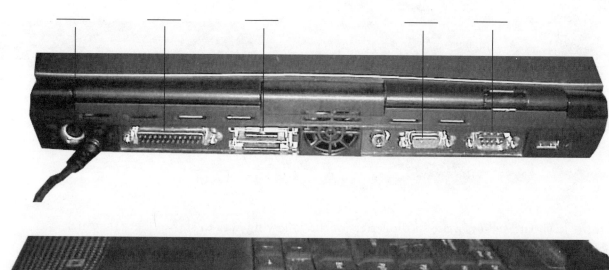

Name: _____

Date: _____

Project 1C: Working with a PDA

Time to Complete: 10 minutes
Needed: A PDA; Web access (optional)
Reference: Pages 20 through 21 of the textbook

1. Turn on your PDA and adjust the screen brightness to an optimal level. Describe where the Brightness control is located on your PDA.

   _____

   _____

2. Experiment with the buttons on the PDA to determine what each button does, and then draw a diagram of the PDA below pointing out each button and its purpose.

3. Open the Notepad (or equivalent) feature on the PDA and try writing your name with the stylus. Refer to the reference material that came with the PDA as needed to learn the writing system. Then, using the PDA's handwriting recognition symbols instead of the regular alphabet, write your full name below.

   _____

4. Go to the Web site for the PDA's manufacturer, and find out how you would install a new application that you had downloaded for the PDA. List the URL and describe the process below.

http://_____

_____

_____

_____

Project 1D: Working with Numbering Systems

Time to Complete: 10 minutes
Needed: A PC running any version of Windows
Reference: Page 4 of the textbook

1. Open the Calculator application in Windows (on the Start/Programs/Accessories menu). Change to Scientific view (View/Scientific).

2. Make sure the Decimal option button is selected. Then key **291**, and click the Bin option button. What is the result?

_____

3. Convert the following numbers from Decimal to Binary.

168 _____
211 _____
05 _____
6412 _____

4. Convert the following numbers from Decimal to Hexadecimal.

15 _____
17 _____
255 _____
10100 _____

5. Convert the following numbers from Binary to Decimal.

0101 _____
1010 _____
11111111 _____
10000001 _____

6. Describe an on-the-job PC technician situation in which you might need to convert between numbering systems.

_____

_____

Project 1E: Becoming More Comfortable Inside a PC

Time to Complete: 10-15 minutes

Needed: A typical PC

Safety: Do not touch any circuit boards inside the PC. Before touching anything inside the PC, touch the metal frame of the PC to avoid shocking any components with static electricity.

Reference: Pages 7 through 19 of the textbook

1. Remove the PC's cover.

2. Locate the ribbon cable that connects the floppy drive to the motherboard. Notice the orientation of the red stripe on the cable; then disconnect it from the floppy drive. How many wires are there in this ribbon cable? *Hint: It is the same as the number of holes in the connector.*

_____

3. What do you think is the purpose of the red stripe on the cable?

_____

4. Reconnect the floppy drive cable to the drive.

5. Locate the power supply connector that attaches the power supply to the floppy drive, and unplug it. Draw a close-up picture of the connector below, including the four wires, and label each wire according to color.

6. Reconnect the power supply cable to the drive.

7. Find the Power LED on the front of the PC, and then look at the inside of the case to see what is behind it. Trace the wires leading from that LED. To what do they connect?

_____

8. Locate the power supply, and read the label on it. What is the wattage of the power supply?

_____

9. Locate the CPU on the motherboard. Do not touch it; just look for now. What, if anything, can you determine about the CPU's type or capacity just by looking?

_____

10. Locate the RAM banks on the motherboard. How many pieces ("sticks") of RAM are installed?

_____

11. Replace the PC's cover.

Name: _____

Date: _____

2 Safety and Preventive Maintenance

As a PC technician, you will not only need to follow safety and cleaning procedures that keep equipment running in top condition, but you will also probably be responsible for advising others about those procedures. Therefore it is essential that you be familiar with them before your first day on the job.

Project 2A: Preparing to Work Safely on a PC

Time to Complete: 10 minutes
Needed: A typical PC; an antistatic wrist strap; Phillips screwdriver (if required to remove PC cover)
Optional: Any additional equipment or materials useful for minimizing ESD
Reference: Pages 34 through 44 of the textbook

1. Locate the fire extinguisher nearest to your workstation.

   a. Approximately how many feet away is it? _____

   b. What classes of fires can it put out? _____

   c. If it is not rated for electrical fires, where is the nearest fire extinguisher that is?

   _____

2. Check your clothing and jewelry to make sure you are not wearing anything that could pose a safety hazard. List three examples of items that might pose a hazard, and tell why they are hazardous.

   _____

   _____

   _____

3. At your workstation, take any steps needed to minimize the risk of ESD.

   a. What does ESD stand for? _____

   b. List three things you can do to a workstation to minimize ESD hazards.

   _____

   _____

   _____

4. Remove the cover on your PC if it is not already off. Demonstrate how to attach your antistatic wrist strap to yourself and to the PC; then remove it from both. On the picture below, draw the cord from the antistatic wrist strap to the PC, showing where you connected the strap's alligator clip to the PC.

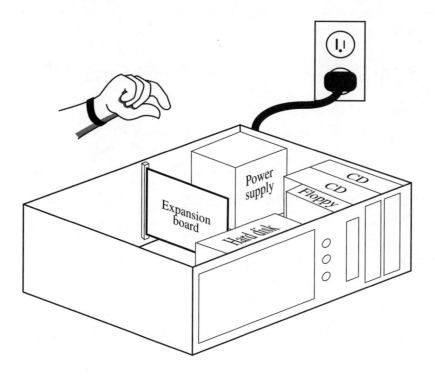

5. Which does the antistatic wrist strap protect from harm: you or the PC?

_____

6. Explain how the antistatic wrist strap works.

_____

_____

_____

7. Describe a situation in which you would not want to use an antistatic wrist strap while working on a PC.

_____

_____

_____

Project 2B: Cleaning a PC

Time to Complete: 15 to 20 minutes
Needed: A typical PC; spray cleaners designed for PCs; soft, dry, lint-free cloths; can of compressed air; cotton swabs; denatured alcohol
Reference: Pages 44 through 49 of the textbook

1. Make sure the PC and monitor are turned off.

2. Clean your PC (the main system unit box) and monitor thoroughly, using appropriate cleaning materials. Describe any special challenges you encountered.

   _____

   _____

3. Describe the cleaning materials you used on each of the following components.

   External surfaces of PC case:_____

   Internal components such as the motherboard: _____

   Monitor glass: _____

4. Thoroughly clean your keyboard. Describe the cleaning supplies you used and the way you used them.

   _____

   _____

   _____

5. Disassemble your mouse or trackball for cleaning. Draw a diagram showing how you disassembled it (what screws you removed, what panels slid back, etc.).

6. Clean your mouse or trackball, and then reassemble it. Describe the cleaning supplies you used and the way you used them.

_____

_____

_____

7. Reassemble any parts of the PC that are still disassembled, and then start up the PC to make sure it still works. Check the mouse or trackball. Describe any problems you ran into and how you solved them.

_____

_____

_____

Project 2C: Cleaning an Inkjet Printer

Time to Complete: 5 to 10 minutes
Needed: A typical inkjet printer, installed on a Windows PC
Reference: Pages 49 through 50 of the textbook

1. Wipe down the outside of the printer with a soft cloth and a spray cleaner designed for PCs.

2. In Windows, run the printer's self-cleaning utility. Describe the steps for doing so.

_____

_____

_____

_____

_____

_____

_____

_____

_____

Project 2D: Cleaning a Laser Printer

Time to Complete: 5 to 10 minutes
Needed: A typical laser printer; any cleaning supplies required for cleaning the specific model, such as cotton swabs and denatured alcohol
Reference: Pages 51 through 52 of the textbook

1. Clean the external surfaces of the printer with a soft cloth and cleaning spray designed for PCs.

2. In the printer's manual (if you have it), find the procedure for cleaning the internal parts of the printer. Give the page number of the manual on which you found this information. _____

   If you do not have the manual, search the Web for information about cleaning your specific printer model's internal parts. Give the URL at which you found the information.

   http://_____

3. Clean your laser printer according to the manufacturer's instructions. List the steps you took.

   _____

   _____

   _____

   _____

   _____

   _____

   _____

   _____

Project 2E: Identifying Hazardous Materials

Time to Complete: 10 minutes
Needed: A typical PC
Reference: Page 52 of the textbook

1. Remove the cover from the PC so you can see inside.

2. Suppose you were going to break down this PC and dispose of it. What parts would need to be taken to a hazardous waste facility rather than thrown in the regular trash?

Part   **Reason for Special Handling**

_____   _____

_____   _____

_____   _____

_____   _____

_____   _____

_____   _____

_____   _____

_____   _____

3. What parts could safely be placed in the regular trash?

_____

_____

_____

_____

_____

4. Of the cleaning supplies you used in project 2B, which should be taken to a hazardous waste facility rather than being thrown in the regular trash?

_____

_____

_____

_____

5. On the Web, locate an MSDS for any of the above-listed hardware or cleaning supplies. Write the URL for it below.

http://_____

3 Case, Electricity, and Power Supplies

The power supply converts standard AC electricity to low-voltage DC current suitable for the use of the electronic components inside the PC, including drives and circuit boards. As a PC technician you will need to diagnose power problems, calculate wattage requirements, measure electrical current using a multimeter, and replace power supplies.

Project 3A: Examining a PC Case

Time to Complete: 10 minutes
Needed: A typical PC
Reference: Pages 62 through 69 of the textbook

1. Circle the area on the following figure where the power supply will be installed.

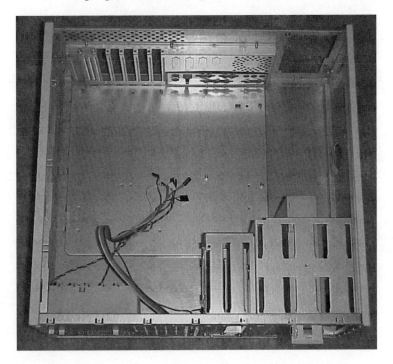

2. What motherboard form factor is this case designed for? How can you tell?

_____

3. How many large external drive bays are there in this case?_____

4. What is the maximum number of expansion slots on a motherboard that this case can support?_____

5. To what component will the wires shown in the photo be attached when the PC is installed in the case?

_____

6. Now look at the case for your own PC, and answer these questions about it.

   a. Is this an AT case or an ATX? _____

   b. How many external drive bays are there? _____

   c. How many are free? _____

   d. Does the case have a removable floor? _____ If so, how many screws would be required to remove in order to take it out? _____

Project 3B: Removing and Reinstalling a Power Supply

Time to Complete: 10 to 20 minutes
Needed: A typical PC; a can of compressed air
Reference: Pages 88 through 89 of the textbook

1. On the following figures, circle the screws to remove in order to take out the power supplies.

2. Remove the cover from your PC if it is not already off, and disconnect the power supply from everything that it is plugged into. List the items from which you unplugged it.

_____

_____

_____

_____

3. Remove the screws holding the power supply in the case, and take it out of the case.

4. With compressed air, clean any visible dust out of the power supply vent holes.

5. Check all connectors for damage, making sure that all wires are securely attached to their connectors and that no pins are bent on the drives and circuit boards to which the power supply connectors attach. If you noticed any problems, list them here.

_____

_____

6. Reinstall the power supply in the case.

7. Reconnect the power supply wires to all the devices you disconnected in step 2. Refer to the list you made in step 2 to make sure you remember all of them.

8. Replace the PC cover and then start up the PC to make sure it works. If you encounter any problems, note them below and troubleshoot as needed.

_____

_____

Project 3C: Installing and Testing a UPS

Time to Complete: 10 to 15 minutes
Needed: A typical PC; a UPS
Reference: Pages 90 through 91 of the textbook

1. On the UPS panel shown below, draw arrows pointing to the outlets that have battery backup.

2. Explain how you knew that the outlets you chose above were battery protected.

_____

_____

3. Suppose you have a UPS that has only three battery-protected outlets, plus three outlets that have surge protection only. You have a monitor, a PC system unit, a network hub, a set of speakers, and a scanner, all of which require electricity. Which three will you pick to have battery backup, and why?

_____

_____

_____

_____

4. Examine your own UPS.

   a. How many battery-protected outlets does it have? _____

   b. How many additional outlets does it have? _____

5. List all the electrical devices associated with your PC, and then circle the ones to which you plan to give the battery backup.

_____

_____

_____

_____

_____

_____

6. Connect the UPS to the wall outlet. Describe the self-test routine it performs.

_____

_____

_____

_____

_____

_____

7. Does it appear to be working correctly after finishing its self-test? How can you tell this?

_____

_____

8. Connect your electrical devices to the UPS using the plan you outlined in step 5.

9. Restart your PC and test all electrical devices to make sure they work. If you have any problems, document them below.

_____

_____

_____

_____

Project 3D: Multimeter Practice

Time to Complete: 20 minutes
Needed: A typical PC; a multimeter; a small battery (such as AA size)
Reference: Pages 73 through 76 of the textbook

1. Plug the cords for the probes into the multimeter—black probe to black socket, red probe to red socket. If there are separate red sockets for volts, amps, and/or current, choose the one for volts.

2. Turn on the multimeter and check to make sure its LED illuminates.

3. Set the multimeter to measure voltage. There may be a dial, a switch, or a button to press.

4. Locate a battery to use for this exercise. It can be any battery that has well-defined positive and negative terminal points, such as a flashlight battery or an AA or AAA battery. Read the battery's label; what is the expected voltage for this battery?_____

5. Touch the red probe to the positive terminal on the battery and the black probe to the negative terminal. What is the voltage reported by the multimeter?_____

6. Suppose you have a motherboard that seems to be "dead." It is installed in a PC, but you are not sure whether the problem is the motherboard itself or the power supply. You want to back-probe the Power_Good wire on the power supply connector to the motherboard.

   a. On an AT system, what color is the Power_Good wire? _____

   b. On an ATX system, what color is the Power_Good wire? _____

   c. What would be an acceptable voltage for the Power_Good wire? _____

7. On the following figure, draw probes showing where the red and black probes would be placed on the power supply connector when checking the Power_Good wire. Make sure you label your probes "RED" and "BLACK."

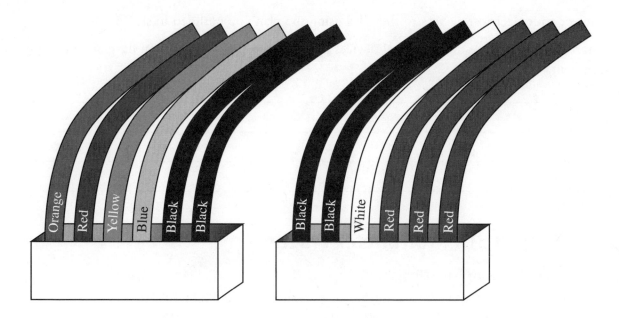

8. On the following figure, is the multimeter dial set correctly for the test described in steps 6 and 7? _____

If not, draw an arrow pointing to the correct setting.

Project 3E: Determining Power Supply Wattage Requirements

Time to Complete: 20 minutes
Needed: A typical PC
Reference: Pages 84 through 86 of the textbook

1. Answer these questions about the power supply label shown below.

```
Model : HP-235ATXAK
AC INPUT (60/50Hz):  115V~/6A ,  230V~/3.5A
DC OUTPUT:    +5V⎓/25A ,  +12V⎓/8A
              −5V⎓/0.5A ,  −12V⎓/0.5A
MAX. OUTPUT POWER: 235W  +3.3V⎓/14A
FUSE RATING: T6.3AH/250V  +5VSB⎓/1A

S / No.  F3- 9 8 0 8 0 3 1 0 0 7

CAUTION! HAZARDOUS AREA
TO AVOID DAMAGING THE POWER SUPPLY,
USE THE CORRECT AC INPUT VOLTAGE RANGE.
TO REDUCE THE RISK OF ELECTRIC SHOCK,
DO NOT REMOVE THIS COVER.
NO SERVICEABLE COMPONENTS INSIDE.
REFER SERVICING TO QUALIFIED SERVICE PERSONNEL.

MADE IN CHINA                              CS
```

a. What type of AC input does this power supply accept?

_____

b. What voltages of output does this power supply generate?

_____

c. Is this a power supply for an AT or an ATX system? How can you tell?

_____

d. How many watts of +5v power can this power supply produce?

_____

e. How many watts of power in total (all voltages) can this power supply produce?

_____

2. Suppose you have a PC with the following components. Some components list their power consumption in terms of amps and volts; others list it in wattage; still others do not provide any information at all.

   Motherboard: 6 amps of +5v and 0.7 amps of +12v
   PCI video card: 5 watts
   Three ISA expansion boards, using 10 watts each
   Floppy drive: 5 watts
   IDE hard drive: 0.6 amps of +5v and 0.5 amps of +12v
   ZIP drive: 0.8 amps of +5v
   CD-ROM drive: 1 amp of +5v and 1.5 amps of +12v
   RAM: 16 watts

   a. What is the total wattage consumed by the above-listed components?_____

   b. Based on the information provided, would the power supply shown in the picture for step 1be adequate for this PC?

   _____

3. Remove the cover from your PC and examine the label on the power supply. Then answer the following questions about it.

   a. What voltages of output does this power supply generate?_____

   b. How many watts of power can this power supply generate in total?_____

   c. How many watts of +12v power can this power supply produce?_____

   d. How many watts of power in total (all voltages) can this power supply produce?_____

   e. There is a red switch on the power supply, near the power cord connector. What is its current setting, and under what circumstances might you need to change that setting?

   _____

   _____

   _____

4. Locate a Web site where you can buy a high-quality replacement power supply for your PC that would provide at least the same wattage as it currently has.

   http://_____

PART 2

Processing and Memory

In this section of the workbook, you have the opportunity to practice selecting, installing, configuring, and troubleshooting the most essential parts of the PC: the motherboard, the CPU, and the memory. You will also demonstrate your ability to enter and make changes to the BIOS Setup. Some of the tasks you will perform include:

- Configuring a motherboard
- Replacing the motherboard battery
- Identifying CPU specifications
- Installing a CPU
- Selecting the appropriate RAM for a motherboard
- Installing RAM
- Examining memory usage
- Fixing a corrupt paging file
- Selecting and installing cable adapters
- Shopping for network cabling
- Working with a pin-out diagram
- Installing a motherboard in a case
- Testing a motherboard
- Accessing BIOS Setup
- Disabling a legacy COM port in BIOS
- Updating a flash BIOS

You will want to make sure you have mastered these skills before you secure a job as a PC technician because the CPU, motherboard, and memory are among the most expensive parts in a computer. Having some practice handling and installing them now can help you avoid expensive on-the-job mistakes later.

4 The Motherboard

The motherboard is the single most important circuit board in a PC. Everything else connects to it. Therefore, when you are adding or replacing parts on a PC, you will almost always interact with the motherboard. The following projects help you refine and demonstrate your understanding of the motherboard.

Project 4A: Identifying Motherboard Features

Time to Complete: 15 to 20 minutes

Needed: A motherboard, either loose or installed in a PC

Optional: Multiple motherboards of different types, for comparison

Reference: Pages 110 through 140 of the textbook

1. Is the following motherboard an AT or an ATX? List at least two ways that you can tell.

    _____

    _____

    _____

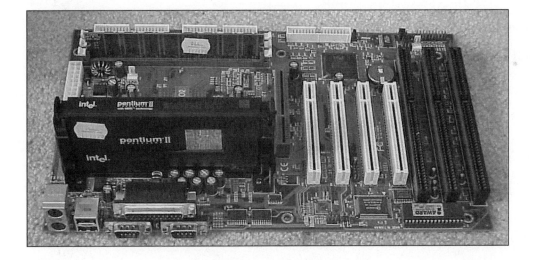

2. Using the letter preceding each part, label the following parts on the motherboard shown above.

    a. CPU
    b. RAM
    c. Power supply connector
    d. AGP slot
    e. PCI slot

    f. ISA slot
    g. COM port
    h. LPT port
    i. BIOS chip
    j. Battery

    k. Keyboard connector
    l. Mouse connector
    m. USB port

3. Examine the motherboard you have to work with in your lab. It may be in a PC, or it may be loose. Answer the following questions.

   a. Is it an AT or an ATX? _____

   b. How many PCI slots does it have? _____

   c. How many SIMM slots? _____

   d. How many DIMM slots? _____

   e. How many ISA slots? _____

   f. What is the chipset make and model? _____

   g. What company manufactured the motherboard? _____

   h. What company manufactured the BIOS? _____

   i. What built-in components does it have (if any), such as video, sound, or network support, and what are the make and model of each? _____

   _____

   _____

4. (Optional) If you have more than one motherboard available to you, answer the following questions about the other motherboard.

   a. Is it an AT or an ATX? _____

   b. What types of local bus does it have? Circle as many as apply:
      VLB   PCI   AGP

   c. How many PCI slots does it have? _____

   d. How many SIMM slots? _____

   e. How many DIMM slots? _____

   f. How many ISA slots? _____

   g. What is the chipset make and model? _____

   h. Is this a Hub or a North/South Bridge chipset? _____

   i. What company manufactured the motherboard? _____

   j. What company manufactured the BIOS? _____

   k. What built-in components does it have (if any), such as video, sound, or network support, and what are the make and model of each? _____

   _____

   _____

Name: _____

Date: _____

Project 4B: Configuring a Motherboard

Time to Complete: 15 to 20 minutes if a manual is available; up to 45 minutes if the information must be found on the Internet
Needed: A motherboard, either loose or installed in a PC; a manual for the motherboard or Web access
Optional: Multiple motherboards of different types, for comparison
Reference: Pages 110 through 140 of the textbook

If the manual is available for the motherboard, consult it to get the following information. If not, look up the motherboard's specifications on the Web using the information gathered in Project 4A, and write the URL where you found the information.

http://_____

1. What CPUs does this motherboard accept? What speeds? _____
   _____

2. How much RAM can it accept, and what type? Include any requirements regarding speed, size, and combinations.

   _____

   _____

3. In the space below, draw a rectangle representing the motherboard, and then draw small rectangles on it representing the individual jumpers. Label each of the jumpers according to their purpose.

4. Pick one of the supported CPU types and speeds and then write it here. _____
List the jumper settings you would need to set on the motherboard to support this CPU.

_____

5. Change the motherboard's jumper settings to match the specifications listed in step 4.

6. (Optional) If you have another motherboard available, repeat the above steps for the second motherboard, and write your answers below.

_____

_____

_____

_____

_____

_____

_____

_____

_____

Drawing for second motherboard:

Project 4C: Replacing the Motherboard Battery

Time to Complete: 5 to 10 minutes
Needed: A motherboard with a coin-style battery; Web access
Reference: Pages 137 through 139, 142 of the textbook

CAUTION

Removing the motherboard battery will cause all the BIOS settings to revert to their default. If you have any special settings configured in BIOS Setup that you want to remember, such as hard disk settings, copy them down before doing this project so you can reset them.

---

1. Locate the battery on the motherboard. Draw a rectangle below representing the motherboard, write "CPU" where the CPU is located, and then draw a circle where the battery is located in relation to the CPU.

2. Remove the battery from the motherboard.

3. Examine the battery, looking for any identification numbers or codes. Write them here.

   _____

4. On the Web, find a Web site where you can buy a replacement for this battery and then record its URL.

   http://_____

5. Put the battery back into the motherboard.

Project 4D: Researching High-End Motherboards

Time to Complete: 15 to 30 minutes
Needed: Web access
Reference: Pages 110 through 140 of the textbook

1. Locate a Web site that has technical reviews and information about the latest high-end motherboards and PCs and then record its URL.

   http://_____

2. Suppose you want to build a dual-CPU PC that uses the fastest CPU available today. What would that CPU be (type and speed)?_____

   Provide a URL for a dual-CPU motherboard that would be suitable for this system.

   http://_____

3. List at least five features of the high-end motherboard you chose in step 2 that are different from a typical consumer-grade PC.

   _____

   _____

   _____

   _____

   _____

   _____

   _____

4. Find an online price comparison shopping site, and find the best price for the motherboard you chose in step 2. What is that price? _____

   Write the URL from which you can buy it at that price.

   http://_____

5 CPUs

The Central Processing Unit (CPU) is the primary chip for processing instructions in the PC. Over the years there have been many CPU sizes, types, and speeds, each designed to work with a specific type of motherboard. In the following projects you will practice selecting and configuring CPUs and getting information about them on the Web.

Project 5A: Identifying CPU Specifications Part 1

Time to Complete: 10 to 15 minutes
Reference: Pages 165 through 190 of the textbook

1. Under the following pictures of CPUs, do the following.
   a. Write A under the PGA CPUs
   b. Write B under the SEC CPUs
   c. Write C under CPUs that are ZIF PGA
   d. Write D under CPUs that operate at an internal speed of 90MHz or higher
   e. Write E under CPUs that are Pentium or higher
   f. Write F under CPUs that are FC (Flip Chip) PGA
   g. Write G under CPUs that are made by Intel

1.

2.

3.

5.

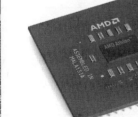

4.

7.

6.

2. For CPUs 1 through 7 above, answer as many of the following questions as possible. Refer to the textbook for specifications on the various CPU types.

   a. Name and manufacturer
   b. Internal speed, or possible range of speeds if exact speed is unknown
   c. Type of motherboard slot it would require

      1) _____

      2) _____

      3) _____

      4) _____

      5) _____

      6) _____

      7) _____

Project 5B: Identifying CPU Specifications Part II

Time to Complete: 10 to 15 minutes
Needed: A CPU, either loose or installed in a motherboard
Optional: Multiple CPUs of different types, for comparison
Reference: Pages 158 through 190 of the textbook

1. Examine your CPU. Write as much information about it as you can.

   _____

   _____

   _____

   _____

2. On the Web, locate three different motherboards in which this CPU would work.
   Write the URLs below.

   http://_____

   http://_____

   http://_____

3. What type of cooling does your CPU require? Write the URL where you found this information.

   http://_____

Project 5C: Changing Motherboard Settings for a New CPU

Time to Complete: 5 to 10 minutes
Reference: Pages 158 through 162 of the textbook

Suppose you have a motherboard imprinted with the following chart showing the settings for jumpers 1 through 7.

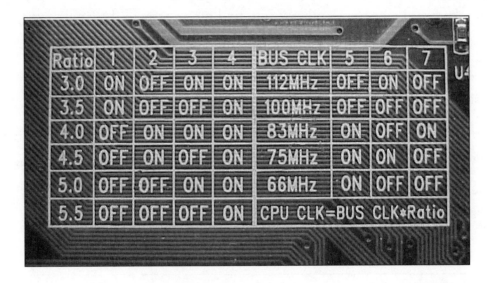

Ratio	1	2	3	4	BUS CLK	5	6	7
3.0	ON	OFF	ON	ON	112MHz	OFF	ON	OFF
3.5	ON	OFF	OFF	ON	100MHz	OFF	OFF	OFF
4.0	OFF	ON	ON	ON	83MHz	ON	OFF	ON
4.5	OFF	ON	OFF	ON	75MHz	ON	ON	OFF
5.0	OFF	OFF	ON	ON	66MHz	ON	OFF	OFF
5.5	OFF	OFF	OFF	ON	CPU CLK=BUS CLK*Ratio			

Next to each CPU speed listed in the table below, write ON or OFF in the columns for each of the jumpers.

CPU Speed	1	2	3	4	5	6	7
200MHz							
233MHz							
333MHz							
450MHz							
560MHz							

Name: _____

Date: _____

Project 5D: Researching the Latest CPUs

Time to Complete: 5 to 10 minutes
Reference: Pages 189 through 190 of the textbook

New CPUs are introduced every year, with new capabilities, higher speeds, and different requirements for cooling and motherboard support. Use the Web to find the answers to these questions.

1. What is the fastest CPU available today, measured in terms of its internal speed (MHz)?

   _____

2. List a Web site where a PC based on the CPU can be purchased.

   http://_____

3. What company manufactures it? _____

4. How many operations per second can it perform? _____

5. What distinguishes this class of CPU from earlier ones? List at least three things.

   _____

   _____

   _____

6. Find a Web site where you can buy this CPU separately (not as part of a whole PC) and write its URL.

   http://_____

7. Find a Web site where you can buy a motherboard compatible with this CPU and write its URL.

   http://_____

6 Memory

There are many types of memory, but the most common type that PC technicians work with is Random-Access Memory (RAM), the "main memory" in a PC. In the following projects you will practice and demonstrate skills such as distinguishing between types of RAM, selecting appropriate RAM for a system, and examining RAM usage through an operating system interface.

Project 6A: Identifying Types of RAM

Time to Complete: 10 to 15 minutes
Reference: Pages 205 through 210 of the textbook

1. Under the pictures of RAM, do the following.

   a. Write A under all the SIMMs
   b. Write B under all the DIMMs
   c. Write C under parity SIMMs

   d. Write D under 72-pin SIMMs
   e. Write E under 30-pin SIMMs

1.

2.

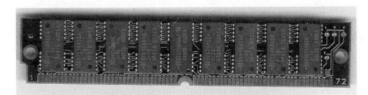

3.

4.

5.

2. What type of RAM packaging would the motherboard in the following photo use? Circle one.

30-pin SIMM   72-pin SIMM   DIMM

3. List at least two clues that you used to arrive at your answer in question 2.

_____

_____

Project 6B: Selecting the Appropriate RAM for a Motherboard

Time to Complete: 15 to 20 minutes
Needed: A typical PC; Web access
Optional: The motherboard's manual
Reference: Pages 205 through 211 of the textbook

1. Locate the RAM banks on your motherboard. Describe the existing RAM installed there.

Physical type (SIMM, DIMM): _____

Number of sticks per bank: _____

Megabytes per stick: _____

Number of full banks: _____

Number of empty banks: _____

RAM speed (if known): _____

Special features of the RAM (if known): _____

_____

2. Many motherboards can accept more than one type of RAM. What additional types of RAM will your motherboard accept besides what is already installed? Get this information from the motherboard manual or from the Web.

_____

_____

_____

If you had to use the Web to find this information, list the URL where you found it.

http://_____

3. Suppose you wanted to double the amount of RAM currently installed in your PC. Describe the RAM you would purchase. Include all the details you would need when shopping for it.

_____

_____

_____

4. Locate a Web site that sells the above-described RAM, and write its URL.

http://_____

5. What would be the total cost, including taxes and shipping, for next-day delivery of the needed RAM? $_____

Project 6C: Examining Memory Usage at a Command Prompt

Time to Complete: 15 to 20 minutes
Needed: A PC with Windows 95 or 98 installed
Reference: Pages 215 through 217 of the textbook

1. Open a command prompt window from within Windows 95 or 98. Write the steps for doing so here.

   _____

   _____

   _____

2. Key **MEM** and then press Enter.

   a. How much conventional memory does your system have in total? _____

   b. What is the largest executable program size? _____

   c. How much available XMS memory? _____

3. Many Windows-based applications are larger than the largest executable program size listed above; explain how Windows makes it possible for them to run.

   _____

   _____

   _____

4. Key **MEM /C | MORE** and then press Enter. List the programs that are loaded into conventional memory and their sizes.

   _____

   _____

   _____

   _____

   _____

   _____

5. Reboot the PC to a command prompt. To do so, press F8 quickly when you see the Starting Windows message on-screen. Then choose the Command Prompt Only option.

6. At the command prompt, key **MEM /C | MORE** and then press Enter. What programs are loaded into conventional memory now?

_____

_____

_____

_____

7. Reboot to a command prompt again, but this time after pressing F8 choose the Safe Mode Command Prompt. What programs are loaded into conventional memory now?

_____

_____

_____

_____

8. Restart Windows normally, and then, from the Start/Shut Down command, restart in MS-DOS mode. What programs are loaded into conventional memory now?

_____

_____

_____

_____

_____

Project 6D: Examining Memory Usage in Windows

Time to Complete: 10 minutes
Needed: A PC with Windows 98, Me, 2000, or XP installed
Reference: Pages 220 through 222 of the textbook

1. From the Control Panel in Windows, double-click System, and then click the General tab. How much RAM is reported there? _____

2. Does this match the amount of RAM you thought the PC had? If not, how do you account for the discrepancy?

    _____

3. Open the System Information utility from the Start menu (Start/Programs/Accessories/System Tools/System Information). From the System Summary, gather the following information.

    Total Physical Memory _____

    Available Physical Memory _____

    Total Virtual Memory _____

    Available Virtual Memory _____

    Page File Space _____

4. Based on your answers to questions 2 and 3 above, what memory does the amount of RAM listed in question 2 refer to? _____

Project 6E: Fixing a Corrupt Paging File in Windows

Time to Complete: 10 minutes
Needed: A PC with Windows 98, Me, 2000, or XP installed
Reference: Pages 221 through 222 of the textbook

For this project, suppose that Windows does not start normally, and you receive an error message about VMM386.VXD being corrupt. This is the paging file in Windows; if it is corrupt, Windows cannot access virtual memory. In this project you will learn how to delete the old, corrupt paging file and create a new one. (It will not hurt anything to do this even though you have not actually experienced the problem.)

Name: _____

Date: _____

1. Reboot Windows in Safe Mode.

2. Disable virtual memory through the System Properties. The exact procedure for doing this varies depending on your Windows version; write the steps that you followed.

_____

_____

_____

_____

_____

_____

_____

_____

3. Reboot Windows normally. Do you notice any difference in Windows' performance? If so, what do you notice?

_____

_____

_____

4. Through the System Properties, reenable virtual memory, and set it up so Windows manages the settings for it automatically.

5. Reboot Windows normally. How is the performance now different from what you noted in step 3?

_____

_____

6. View the virtual memory settings again through System Properties. What has Windows chosen as the paging file size? _____

7 Cables

Whenever you need to connect two pieces of hardware, a cable is required. There are dozens of cable types that a PC technician needs to be able to recognize and select intelligently, such as ribbon cables, printer cables, USB cables, and so on. In this section you will demonstrate your knowledge of cable types and usage.

Project 7A: Identifying Cable Types

Time to Complete: 10 minutes
Reference: Pages 232 through 257 of the textbook

Write the specified information next to each cable photo below.

1. How many wires are in this cable? _____

2. Is this a parallel or serial cable? _____

3. What type of device would this cable plug into? _____

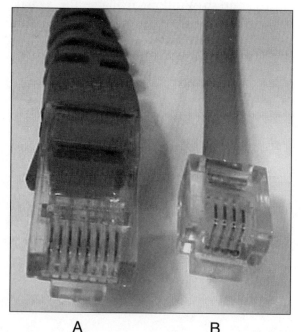

A   B

4. Which connector, A or B, would plug into a modem?

   _____

5. Which connector, A or B, would plug into a 10BaseT Ethernet card? _____

6. How many wires does connector A have? _____

7. What is the common name for connector A?

   _____

8. Is this a parallel or a serial cable? _____

9. Which end connects to the PC: male or female? _____

10. Give an example of a device that would use this cable. _____

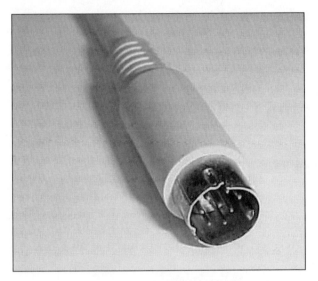

11. What is the common name for this type of connector? _____

12. On an ATX system, name two devices that use this connector. _____

13. On an AT system, name one device that uses this connector. _____

14. What type of connector is this? _____

15. What is the most common type of device that uses this connector? _____

16. How many pins are in the D-sub connector at the other end of this cable? _____

17. What port on a PC does the other end of this cable plug into? _____

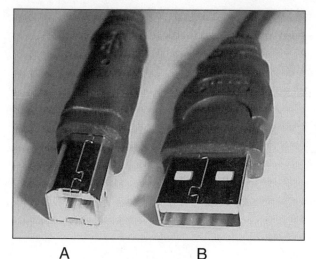

A   B

18. A and B are opposite ends of the same cable. What type of cable is it? _____

19. Which end, A or B, connects to the PC? _____

20. Give an example of a device that would use this cable. _____

21. Which of the connectors shown in this project will plug directly into your PC without the need for any adapters, converters, or add-on boards? Place a check mark next to each of them that will.

Project 7B: Selecting and Installing Cable Adapters

Time to Complete: 10 minutes
Reference: Pages 242 through 252 of the textbook

1. In the following sentences, fill in the blanks with the correct connector type. Choose from the following list of terms. (Some terms may be used more than once; some may not be used at all.)

DB-9 female	DB-25 male	DIN female
DB-9 male	PS/2 female	DIN male
DB-25 female	PS/2 male	RJ-45 male

a. To connect an external modem with a 25-pin connector to a 9-pin serial port on a PC, use a connector with _____ on one side and _____ on the other.

b. To patch together two 25-pin serial cables, use a connector with _____ on one side and _____ on the other.

c. To adapt a keyboard from an ATX system for use on an AT system, use a connector with _____ on one side and _____ on the other.

d. To adapt a serial mouse for use in a PS/2 mouse port, use a connector with _____ on one side and _____ on the other.

e. To connect two PCs together via their parallel ports, start with a parallel cable with straight pass-through wiring. If both ends are already _____, it is ready to use. If not, put an adapter on the _____ end of the cable that converts that end to

_____.

Project 7C: Shopping for Network Cabling

Time to Complete: 15 minutes
Needed: Web access
Reference: Pages 252 through 257 of the textbook

1. What type of cable do you need for a 10Base2 Ethernet network?

   _____

2. Locate a Web site where you can buy the cabling you listed above, and write its URL here.

   http://_____

3. How much will 200 feet of this cable cost at the Web site you listed in step 2?

   _____

4. What type of cable do you need for a 100BaseT Ethernet network?

   _____

5. Locate a Web site where you can buy this cabling, and write its URL here.

   http://_____

6. Suppose you want to connect five PCs to a central hub with 100BaseT Ethernet, and you need to buy five 50-foot cables. How much will this cost at the Web site you listed in step 5?

   _____

7. Suppose you find a good deal on UTP Cat6 cable. Can you use it for a 100BaseT Ethernet network?

   _____

Project 7D: Working with a Pin-Out Diagram

Time to Complete: 10 minutes

Needed: A multimeter; a serial cable with a DB-9 connector on one end and a DB-25 connector on the other

Reference: Pages 235 through 236 of the textbook

1. Familiarize yourself with the procedure for checking the continuity of a cable wire with a multimeter:
   a. Set the multimeter to ohms (resistance).
   b. If your probes are too big to fit into the holes in the female end of the cable, stick the end of an unfolded paper clip into the hole you are testing, and then touch the probe to it. Alternatively you can buy a smaller set of probes.
   c. Touch one probe to the paper clip, or stick it into the hole if possible. At the other end of the cable, touch the other probe to the pin that corresponds to that hole. If resistance of 20 ohms or less is measured, a signal can pass through the wire.

2. Examine the following pin-out diagram for the 9-pin end of a serial cable.

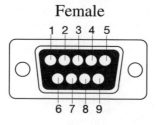
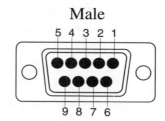

1	Carrier Detect
2	Receive Data
3	Transmit Data
4	Data Terminal Ready
5	Signal Ground
6	Data Set Ready
7	Request to Send
8	Clear to Send
9	Ring Indicator

3. Using your multimeter, determine which of the pins (or holes) on the 25-pin end of the cable correspond to the nine pins listed above, and label them on the following diagram with the names from the right-hand column in the above table.

8 Installing and Troubleshooting the Basic Components

Not only must a competent PC technician know how to select components such as memory, motherboards, and CPUs, but he or she must also be able to assemble them into a usable PC. The projects in this section test your ability to do that.

Project 8A: Installing a PGA-Style CPU in a Motherboard

Time to Complete: 5 to 10 minutes
Needed: A motherboard; a compatible ZIF PGA CPU that is not currently installed in it
Reference: Pages 276 through 280 of the textbook

1. Take appropriate precautions to avoid ESD damage to the CPU as you install it. What precautions will you take?

   _____

   _____

   _____

2. How many pins are there on the CPU you are installing? _____

3. What is the model and speed of this CPU? _____

4. Make sure the motherboard will support this CPU. Explain how you checked this.

   _____

   _____

5. The CPU must be oriented correctly in the slot. On the picture below, draw a line between the corner of the CPU and the corner of the socket that must be aligned.

6. Check the jumpers on the motherboard to make sure they are set correctly for this CPU. Where did you find this information? What are the correct jumper settings?

_____

_____

_____

_____

7. Lift the handle on the CPU socket, insert the CPU, and lower the handle.

8. Determine what type of heat sink or fan this CPU requires. Write its requirements below, and tell where you found the information.

_____

_____

9. Attach an appropriate heat sink or fan to the CPU. Explain how it attaches.

_____

_____

Project 8B: Installing an SEC-Style CPU in a Motherboard

Time to Complete: 5 to 10 minutes
Needed: A motherboard; a compatible SEC-style CPU that is not currently installed in it; support brackets if they are not already attached to the motherboard
Reference: Pages 280 through 282 of the textbook

1. Take appropriate precautions to avoid ESD damage to the CPU as you install it. What precautions will you take?

_____

_____

_____

2. What are the model and speed of this CPU? _____

3. Does the motherboard have a Slot 1 or a Slot A? How do you know?

_____

_____

4. If support brackets are not yet installed around the CPU slot, install them, and document the procedure you followed. If they are already installed, explain how they attach to the motherboard.

_____

_____

_____

_____

5. Check the jumpers on the motherboard to make sure they are set correctly for this CPU. Where did you find this information? What are the correct jumper settings?

_____

_____

_____

_____

6. Insert the CPU into the slot and into the support brackets. Explain how you knew which direction to insert it.

_____

_____

7. Determine what type of heat sink or fan this CPU requires. Write its requirements below, and tell where you found the information.

_____

_____

8. Attach an appropriate heat sink or fan to the CPU. Explain how it attaches.

_____

_____

Project 8C: Installing RAM in a Motherboard

Time to Complete: 5 to 10 minutes

Needed: A motherboard; compatible RAM that is not already installed

Reference: Pages 282 through 285 of the textbook

1. What type of RAM does this motherboard require? How do you know?

   _____

   _____

   _____

   _____

2. What type of RAM do you have? Will it work in this motherboard?

   _____

   _____

3. Is your RAM in the form of SIMMs or DIMMs? _____

4. Install the RAM in the motherboard. In the space below, draw a picture showing the installation process and label it with descriptions of each step.

Project 8D: Installing a Motherboard in a Case

Time to Complete: 15 to 30 minutes

Needed: A motherboard; a case; stand-offs; screws; paper washers; a small Phillips screwdriver

Reference: Pages 285 through 294 of the textbook

1. Confirm that the motherboard is compatible with the case you have. How can you tell?

   _____

   _____

   _____

2. Prepare the case as needed to receive the motherboard. This may include installing brass stand-offs, installing the case speaker, removing the case floor, or other activities. Document below the preparations you made.

   _____

   _____

   _____

   _____

   _____

   _____

3. How many brass stand-offs will installing this motherboard require? _____

   How many plastic stand-offs, if any? _____

4. Install the motherboard in the case, and secure it with screws and paper washers. Document below any problems you had and how you resolved them.

   _____

   _____

   _____

   _____

   _____

   _____

5. Attach the case wires to the motherboard. Draw a diagram below showing the grid of pins on the motherboard to which the wires attach and showing where each connector plugged in.

6. If the motherboard is an AT model, attach the mouse, COM, and LPT ports to the motherboard and to the case. Why is this not necessary on an ATX motherboard?

    _____

7. Connect the power supply to the motherboard.

Project 8E: Testing Motherboard Installation

Prerequisite: Project 8D
Time to Complete: 5 to 30 minutes, depending on problems encountered
Needed: Motherboard and case from project 8D
Reference: Pages 294 through 298 of the textbook

1. Install a video card in the motherboard.

    a. What type of video card is it? _____

    b. What slot does it fit into? _____

2. Connect a monitor to the video card.
3. Connect an AC power cord to the PC's power supply and then plug it into a wall outlet.
4. Turn on the monitor.
5. Turn on the PC.

6. What text do you see on screen? Copy it below and then turn off the PC.

_____

_____

_____

_____

_____

_____

_____

7. If you did not see any text in question 6, troubleshoot and then document your steps below.

_____

_____

_____

_____

_____

_____

_____

_____

_____

Project 8F: Swapping Motherboards

Challenge

Time to Complete: 15 to 30 minutes
Needed: Two cases with motherboards installed, both of the same form factor
Reference: Pages 285 through 295 of the textbook

1. Examine the two cases and motherboards. Is there any physical reason that they might not be interchangeable? If so, note it below.

_____

_____

_____

2. Assuming there is no major incompatibility between the two systems, remove the motherboards from both cases. Note below any problems that you encountered.

    _____

    _____

    _____

    _____

    _____

3. Install the motherboards in the opposite cases. Note any idiosyncrasies, problems, or modifications that were required.

    _____

    _____

    _____

    _____

    _____

4. Completely connect both motherboards to the new cases, and install video cards. Then test each one to make sure it works. Document any problems you encountered.

    _____

    _____

    _____

    _____

    _____

9 Working with the BIOS Setup Program

The BIOS Setup program, sometimes called CMOS Setup, is a technician's gateway to the motherboard's low-level settings. Through the BIOS Setup program you can instruct the motherboard to boot in a certain way, to recognize certain hardware devices, to use power-saving settings or not, and much more. In the following projects you will experiment with the BIOS Setup program built into your PC's motherboard, and demonstrate how you can change some of its basic settings.

Project 9A: Accessing BIOS Setup

Time to Complete: 10 to 15 minutes
Needed: A working PC
Reference: Pages 310 through 313 of the textbook

1. Based on the following figure, what key should you press to enter the BIOS Setup program?

   _____

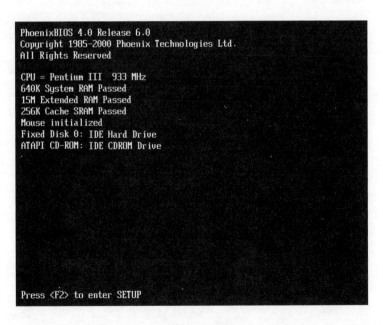

```
PhoenixBIOS 4.0 Release 6.0
Copyright 1985-2000 Phoenix Technologies Ltd.
All Rights Reserved

CPU = Pentium III  933 MHz
640K System RAM Passed
15M Extended RAM Passed
256K Cache SRAM Passed
Mouse initialized
Fixed Disk 0: IDE Hard Drive
ATAPI CD-ROM: IDE CDROM Drive




Press <F2> to enter SETUP
```

2. Power up your PC, and read the text on-screen to determine which key you should press to enter BIOS Setup. When you see the message, immediately press the key. If BIOS Setup does not open (i.e., if Windows starts instead), restart and try again.

3. What key did you press to enter BIOS Setup on your PC? _____

4. Does the mouse work in your BIOS Setup program? _____

5. Examine the instructions on-screen that tell you how to move around in the BIOS Setup program.

    a. What key(s) must you press to move from one setting to another?

_____

    b. What key(s) must you press to change the value for a setting?

_____

    c. What key must you press to get help?

_____

    d. What key must you press to exit the BIOS Setup program?

_____

6. Some BIOS Setup programs, like the one shown below, have multiple menus or "pages" of settings. On the figure below, circle the on-screen instructions that tell how to move from one menu to another.

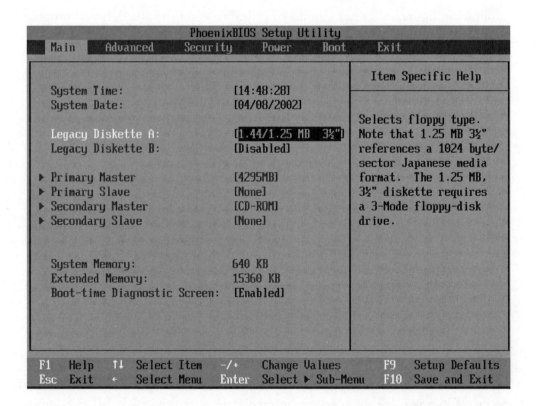

7. What are the names of the menus available in your BIOS Setup program?

_____

_____

_____

_____

_____

_____

8. What key(s) do you press to move to a different menu? _____

9. Locate the System Date setting in your BIOS Setup program, and change it to tomorrow's date.

   a. What menu was the System Date setting found on? _____

   b. What key did you press (or what icon did you click) to make the date editable?

   _____

   c. What date did you enter as the new date? _____

   d. After keying the new date, what key did you press (or what mouse action did you take) to confirm your new setting? _____

10. Change the System Date back to today's date.

11. Locate the System Time setting, and advance the time one hour.

   a. What key did you press (or what icon did you click) to make the time editable?

   _____

   b. While keying the new time, what key did you press to move between the hour, minute, and second fields? _____

   c. After keying the new time, what key did you press (or what mouse action did you take) to confirm your new setting? _____

12. Change the System Time back to the current time.

13. Exit the BIOS Setup program, discarding the changes you have made. Describe the keyboard or mouse actions you took to do this.

_____

_____

_____

_____

_____

_____

Project 9B: Disabling a Legacy Serial Port

Time to Complete: 10 to 15 minutes
Needed: A working PC
Reference: Pages 324 through 325 of the textbook

1. Look on the back of your PC and identify a legacy serial port that is not in use. A legacy serial port is a serial port with a DB-9 or DB-25 male connector on the PC. High-speed serial ports such as USB do not count. Which serial port did you select? (for example, COM1, COM2)

   _____

> ─ N O T E ──
>
> In step 1, if all serial ports are in use, identify a serial port that is being used by a noncritical piece of hardware.
> Examples of noncritical hardware include a PDA interface, an external modem, or a battery backup (UPS).
> Do not choose a serial port that has a mouse attached to it, or you will have difficulty moving around in
> Windows when it is disabled.

2. Enter the BIOS Setup program for your PC.
3. Locate the setting for the chosen serial port, and disable it. Describe below the steps you took to do so.

   _____

   _____

   _____

   _____

   _____

4. Exit the BIOS Setup program, saving your changes.
5. Start Windows and then open Device Manager. Refer to pages 258–259 of the textbook if you need help doing this.
6. Examine the list of ports in Device Manager. Does the disabled port appear on the list? If no, why not? If yes, does it have any special icon or status indicating it is disabled?

   _____

   _____

   _____

   _____

7. Restart the PC and then reenter BIOS Setup. Reenable the disabled COM port. Describe the steps you took to do so.

_____

_____

_____

_____

_____

8. Exit the BIOS Setup program, saving your changes.

9. Start Windows and then open Device Manager. Does the reenabled port appear on the list? If no, why not? If yes, what is its status?

_____

_____

_____

_____

10. Why might it be useful to disable a COM port on a user's system?

_____

_____

_____

_____

Project 9C: Examining Power Management Settings

Time to Complete: 5 to 10 minutes
Needed: A working PC that has a BIOS that supports power management
Reference: Pages 326 through 328 of the textbook

1. Enter your PC's BIOS Setup program, and locate the Power settings.

2. What is the current power management setting? _____

3. What are the other available settings?

_____

_____

_____

_____

_____

4. Does the BIOS Setup program indicate whether it supports APM or ACPI?
   If so, which does it support?

_____

_____

_____

5. Does the BIOS support Wake on Ring? _____

6. Does the BIOS support Wake on LAN? _____

> ## N O T E
> Different BIOS Setup programs call features by different names; yours might use slightly different language for the settings in questions 5 and 6. For example, Wake on Ring might be called Resume on Modem Ring.

7. Of all the settings you wrote down in question 3, which would conserve the most power?

_____

8. Which would offer the best performance?

_____

9. Choose the Power settings that you think are most appropriate for your situation. Write your choices below and explain why you chose them.

_____

_____

_____

_____

10. Exit the BIOS Setup program, saving your changes. If you run into any performance problems with the PC later, change the setting back to its original value (see question 2).

Project 9D: Updating a Flash BIOS

Time to Complete: 5 to 10 minutes

Needed: A working PC that has a BIOS that supports power management

Reference: Pages 331 through 332 of the textbook

Installing an update to a BIOS can add more features to the BIOS Setup program than were originally present. In some cases it can also correct problems such as lockups at startup or shutdown.

> ┌─ C A U T I O N ───────────────────────────────
> This project, if performed incorrectly, can potentially disable the motherboard. Make very sure that you have acquired the correct BIOS update for the motherboard. Follow the instructions exactly. If there is a conflict between the instructions that came with the update and the instructions shown here, give preference to the ones that came with the update because they are more tailored to your individual situation.

1. Identify your current BIOS model and version number. To do so, watch the screen as the PC boots up. At the very beginning of the boot process, the BIOS information appears at the top of the screen. Press the Pause key on the keyboard to pause the boot process and then write down the complete BIOS name and code here.

   _____

   _____

2. On the Web, find an update for this BIOS. A likely place to start looking is the Web site for the PC's manufacturer. Write the URL for the site.

   http://_____

3. If you did not find an update for your BIOS, stop here. Do not settle for an update for anything other than the exact BIOS you have, or it could disable the motherboard.

4. If you did find an update, download the update. It should be an executable (exe) file that creates a bootable floppy disk when run. If the instructions indicate otherwise, follow the instructions rather than relying on this workbook.

> ┌─ N O T E ───────────────────────────────
> Students who have an instructor available may wish to have the instructor verify that the update found is correct for the motherboard, as an additional safety check.

5. Boot the PC from the floppy disk, and follow the on-screen instructions to update the BIOS. Do *not* turn the PC off while the update is occurring.

┌─ C A U T I O N ──
│ Because the motherboard can be ruined if it loses power during a brief but critical phase in the update process, do
│ not perform BIOS updates when there is danger of a power outage, such as during a thunderstorm or during an
│ electricity shortage when a blackout is a possibility.
└──

PART 3

Data Storage

This section covers many types of data storage devices, including floppy disks, hard disks, and numerous types of CDs. You will practice selecting the right disk drive for a task, setting up drives in a PC, partitioning and formatting disks, and managing drives in the operating system. This section also includes device resource assignment (such as IRQs and I/O addresses). Some of the skills you will demonstrate are:

- Configuring drives in BIOS Setup
- Determining a drive's capacity and other properties
- Understanding drive size limitations based on BIOS and OS versions
- Setting master/slave status for IDE drives
- Setting SCSI ID and termination
- Write-protecting a floppy disk
- Partitioning and formatting disks
- Enabling real-mode CD drive support
- Adding CD support to a Windows 95 startup disk
- Writing to CD-R and CD-RW discs
- Examining device resource assignments in Device Manager
- Disabling, removing, and reinstalling device drivers
- Installing Plug-and-Play devices
- Installing non-Plug-and-Play devices
- Manually changing a device's resource assignments

Disk storage is an important set of skills to master because often the data stored on a disk is much more valuable than the disk itself. If you know how to configure, use, and troubleshoot disk drives, you will be able to support your clients in keeping their data safe.

10 Introduction to Disk Storage

Data is stored on disks, which can be either optical (as with CDs and DVDs) or magnetic (as with hard and floppy disks).

Project 10A: Adding a CD Drive in BIOS Setup

Time to Complete: 10 to 15 minutes
Needed: A working PC with at least one free IDE position
Reference: Pages 357 through 360 of the textbook

1. Enter the BIOS Setup program. What key(s) did you press to enter it? _____

2. Locate the settings for IDE devices. Write the current settings in the blanks.

   Primary Master _____

   Primary Slave _____

   Secondary Master _____

   Secondary Slave _____

3. Choose one of the IDE device channels listed in step 2 that is currently set to None or Disabled. What are the choices of values for that IDE position?

   _____

   _____

   _____

   _____

4. Change the setting for that IDE channel to CD-ROM (if available) or ATAPI (if CD-ROM is not one of the choices). Write the steps you used to make this change.

   _____

   _____

   _____

   _____

   _____

   _____

   _____

5. Exit BIOS Setup, saving your changes.

6. Watch the screen as the PC reboots. Do you see any error messages, since BIOS expects there to be a CD-ROM drive but you do not have one physically installed? If so, what is the error message?

_____

_____

_____

7. Reenter BIOS Setup and restore the IDE channel's settings to the original value (which you wrote down in step 2).

8. Exit the BIOS Setup program, saving your changes.

Project 10B: Manually Configuring a Hard Drive in BIOS Setup

Time to Complete: 10 to 15 minutes
Needed: A working PC with at least one free IDE position
Reference: Pages 361 through 366 of the textbook

1. Suppose you have the following information for a drive: the number of cylinders (C), the number of heads (H), the number of sectors per track (S), and the number of bytes stored in each sector (512). Write a formula below showing how to use those numbers to calculate the drive's capacity.

_____

2. What would be the capacity, in gigabytes, for a disk with the specifications shown in the following picture? _____

3. Enter the BIOS Setup program on your PC.

4. Do the following.
    a. Display the settings for the IDE devices.
    b. Choose a free IDE position (one that has no physical device associated with it in the PC, probably set to None or Disabled), and set it to User or Manual. Enter the settings for the hard drive specified in step 2.
    c. Does the BIOS calculate the same capacity for the drive that you manually calculated in step 2? If not, why?

    _____

5. What are the other configurable settings for this drive, and what are their default values? (For example, can you select an LBA mode? A DMA/PIO mode? Can you turn on/off 32-bit disk access?) What other values are available besides the default for each setting?

    _____

    _____

    _____

    _____

    _____

    _____

    _____

    _____

6. Exit the BIOS Setup program, discarding your changes.

Project 10C: Adding a Second Floppy Drive in BIOS Setup

Time to Complete: 5 to 10 minutes
Needed: A working PC with a single floppy drive
Reference: Pages 358 through 359 of the textbook

1. Enter the BIOS Setup program for your PC.

2. Locate the settings for floppy drives. In the blanks, write the current drives' settings.

    Diskette A _____

    Diskette B _____

3. Diskette B is probably set to None or Disabled. Set its value to 3.5-inch 1.44MB. The exact steps for doing this depend on your BIOS Setup program; write the steps you took.

_____

_____

_____

_____

_____

_____

4. Exit BIOS Setup, saving your changes.

5. Watch the screen as the PC reboots. Do you see any error messages about drive B, since BIOS expects there to be a second floppy disk but you do not have one physically installed? If so, what is the error message?

_____

_____

_____

6. Reenter BIOS Setup and restore the floppy drive settings to those that you wrote down in step 2.
7. Exit the BIOS Setup program, saving your changes.

Project 10D: Examining Drive Properties at a Command Prompt

Time to Complete: 5 to 10 minutes
Needed: A working PC with a working hard disk; access to a command prompt (either an MS-DOS prompt or a command prompt from within Windows)
Reference: Pages 366 through 370 of the textbook

1. Display a command prompt by completing the following steps.
   • In MS-DOS, start up the computer. A command prompt appears.
   • In Windows 9x, choose Start and then Run. Key **command** and then click OK.
   • In Windows 2000/XP, choose Start and then Run. Key **cmd** and then click OK.
2. Change to the primary hard drive by keying **C:** and then pressing Enter.

3. Key **CHKDSK** and then press Enter. Wait for it to finish executing. Depending on the Windows version and the file system in use, it may finish almost instantly or there may be a wait of several minutes while it checks the drive.

4. Fill in the blanks below based on the information that appears:

    a. What is the file system in use (FAT, FAT32, NTFS)? _____

    b. What is the volume serial number? _____

    c. What is the allocation unit size? _____

    d. How many allocation units are there, in total, on the disk? _____

    e. What is the total disk space? _____

    f. How much disk space is available? _____

5. (Optional) If you have more than one hard disk partition, change to it by keying its drive letter and a colon—for example, **D:**—and then pressing Enter. Then run CHKDSK on the drive and record its information.

    a. What is the file system in use (FAT, FAT32, NTFS)? _____

    b. What is the volume serial number? _____

    c. What is the allocation unit size? _____

    d. How many allocation units are there, in total, on the disk? _____

    e. What is the total disk space? _____

    f. How much disk space is available? _____

6. Refer in the textbook to Tables 10.1, 10.2, and 10.3 (pages 369–370). Does the allocation unit size reported by CHKDSK for each drive you checked match what you would expect for that drive based on these tables? If not, explain the discrepancies that you found

    _____

    _____

    _____

    _____

    _____

Project 10E: Using a Large Hard Disk with an Old PC

Time to Complete: 10 minutes

Reference: Pages 361 through 364 of the textbook

1. Suppose you just bought a new 20GB hard drive. You install it in an old PC, but the BIOS autodetects it as a 528MB drive. What is happening, and what can you do, if anything, to make the BIOS see it as a larger size?

    _____

    _____

    _____

    _____

    _____

2. Now suppose you have the same new 20GB hard drive; you install it in another older PC (not quite as old as the one in step 1), and the BIOS autodetects it as an 8GB drive. What is happening, and what could you do, if anything, to make the BIOS see it as a larger size?

    _____

    _____

    _____

    _____

    _____

3. You have managed to make the BIOS recognize the drive as its full 20GB, and you are ready to partition and format it. You boot from a Windows 95 startup disk and use FDISK to partition the drive, but it will not let you create partitions larger than 2GB. What is causing this problem, and what can you do to solve it?

    _____

    _____

    _____

    _____

    _____

Disk Drive Interfaces

Integrated Drive Electronics, or IDE, is the most popular interface for hard drives, CD-ROM drives, and a variety of other drives. Its closest competitor is Small Computer Systems Interface, or SCSI, used in high-end systems and file servers. A PC technician must know how to install, configure, and troubleshoot both of these interfaces. In this set of projects you will demonstrate your ability to do that.

Project 11A: Setting IDE Master/Slave Jumpers

Time to Complete: 5 to 10 minutes
Needed: An IDE hard drive
Reference: Pages 392 through 394 of the textbook

1. Suppose that the following chart appears on a hard drive's label.

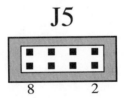

J5

8   2

	J5 (7-8)	J5 (5-6)	J5 (3-4)	J5 (1-2)
ATA Master Only				
ATA Slave	▮			
ATA Master with Slave		▮		
Cable Select	▮	▮		

Name: _____

Date: _____

On the following pictures, draw the jumper cap where it should be positioned.

a. Primary master with no slave:

b. Secondary master with no slave:

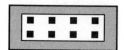

c. Primary master with slave:

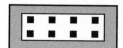

d. Secondary master with slave:

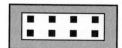

e. Primary slave:

f. Secondary slave:

g. Cable Select:

2. Now suppose that there is no label on the drive, but there are some letters above the jumpers themselves, as shown below.

Chapter 11

On the following diagrams, draw the jumper positions needed.

a. Primary master with no slave:

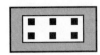

b. Secondary master with no slave:

c. Primary master with slave:

d. Secondary master with slave:

e. Primary slave:

f. Secondary slave:

g. Cable Select:

3. On your own hard drive, what are the choices for jumper settings? In the space below, reproduce the chart from the drive's label, or create your own chart that shows how to set the jumpers for various situations.

Name: _____

Date: _____

Project 11B: Setting SCSI ID and Termination

Time to Complete: 5 to 10 minutes
Optional: A SCSI hard drive
Reference: Pages 397 through 399 of the textbook

Suppose you have a SCSI hard drive with the following chart in the manual that accompanies it.

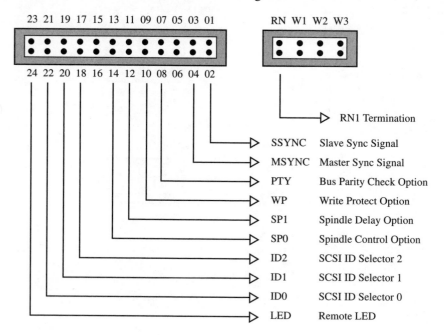

SCSI ID	ID2	ID1	ID0	
0	N	N	N	
1	N	N	Y	
2	N	Y	N	
3	N	Y	Y	
4	Y	N	N	
5	Y	N	Y	
6	Y	Y	N	
7	Y	Y	Y	(default)

Termination Power

W1	On-board local termination power (default)
W2	Termination power via interface cable
W1, W3	Termination power from both locations

1. Draw the jumpers for setting the drive to SCSI ID 6.

23 21 19 17 15 13 11 09 07 05 03 01

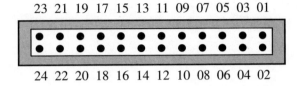

24 22 20 18 16 14 12 10 08 06 04 02

2. Draw the jumpers for setting the drive to SCSI ID 1.

23 21 19 17 15 13 11 09 07 05 03 01

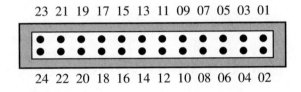

24 22 20 18 16 14 12 10 08 06 04 02

3. Draw the jumpers for setting the drive to SCSI ID 5.

23 21 19 17 15 13 11 09 07 05 03 01

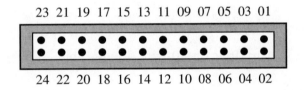

24 22 20 18 16 14 12 10 08 06 04 02

4. Draw the jumpers for on-board powered termination.

RN W1 W2 W3

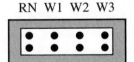

5. (Optional) If you have a SCSI drive available, set it up to be terminated on-board and to use SCSI ID 7. In the space below, draw a rectangle representing the drive, and then draw and label the jumpers and their settings.

Project 11C: Installing an IDE Drive

Time to Complete: 10 to 20 minutes
Needed: An IDE drive (hard, CD, or DVD); a PC with at least one IDE interface free
Reference: Pages 402 through 407 of the textbook

1. Suppose you have a PC that already has the following drives installed:

Primary master: UltraATA/33 hard drive on 40-wire ribbon cable
Primary slave: empty
Secondary master: DVD drive
Secondary slave: CD-RW drive

You plan to install a second hard drive, an UltraATA/100 drive. You can either install it in the primary slave spot on the existing cable, or you can install a new cable. You can leave the other drives in their current positions, or you can shift them around. Determine what arrangement would offer the best overall performance for the system, and explain your decision.

_____

_____

_____

_____

_____

_____

2. On the picture below, draw arrows pointing to the two IDE interface connectors.

3. Now turn to your own PC and evaluate the already-installed IDE devices and the new drive that you will be installing. Based on the capabilities and needs of the new drive, are there any special positioning requirements to consider? For example, should it be on its own IDE cable? Does it need to avoid sharing a cable with certain already-installed drives?

_____

_____

_____

_____

4. Make any changes needed to the existing IDE drive jumper settings and cable connections. Explain the changes you made.

_____

_____

_____

_____

5. Set the new drive's jumpers. What jumper setting did you use?

   _____

6. Install the new drive in an appropriate bay. What type of bay did you choose?

   _____

7. Connect a power cable and a ribbon cable to the new drive. Make sure the red stripe of the ribbon cable is oriented to Pin 1 on the connector. If needed, connect the other end of the ribbon cable to the motherboard.

8. Replace the PC's cover, and start up the PC. Does the BIOS automatically recognize the new drive? How can you tell?

   _____

   _____

   _____

   _____

9. Enter BIOS Setup. If needed, run the BIOS Setup's AutoDetect IDE utility. What settings does it detect for the new drive? Do they match the settings on the drive's label?

   _____

   _____

   _____

   _____

10. If the BIOS Setup does not see the new drive, troubleshoot the problem and describe your troubleshooting steps.

    _____

    _____

    _____

    _____

Name: _____

Date: _____

Project 11D: Installing a SCSI Interface Card and Hard Drive

Time to Complete: 10 to 20 minutes
Needed: A SCSI hard drive; a SCSI adapter board
Reference: Pages 399 through 407 of the textbook

1. Examine the SCSI adapter board. What is its current SCSI ID setting? How can you tell?

   _____

   _____

2. What is the board's current termination setting? How can you tell?

   _____

   _____

3. Identify an appropriate expansion slot in the motherboard in which to install the SCSI adapter board, and then install the adapter in it. Describe the steps you took.

   _____

   _____

   _____

   _____

   _____

   _____

   _____

4. Examine the SCSI hard drive. What is its current SCSI ID setting? _____

   If it is the same as the SCSI adapter, change it, and explain below how you did it and what the new ID is.

   _____

   _____

   _____

5. Is the SCSI hard drive terminated? Should it be? Set the termination setting appropriately, and explain below what setting you used and how you set it.

_____

_____

_____

6. Install the hard drive in the PC case, in any available drive bay of an appropriate size. Connect the power supply to the drive.

7. Connect the hard drive to the SCSI adapter board. Describe the cable you used for this. How many pins does it have? Does it use a DB connector? Centronics? Some other type? How many connectors does it have on it?

_____

_____

_____

_____

_____

_____

8. Replace the PC cover, and start up the PC. Watch the screen for information about the SCSI adapter and/or the SCSI hard drive. If needed, press the Pause key to freeze the screen so you can have more time to read it. Document what you saw.

_____

_____

_____

_____

_____

Project 11E: Shopping for Add-On IDE Controller Boards

Time to Complete: 10 to 20 minutes

Needed: Web access

Reference: Pages 386 through 392 of the textbook

The latest IDE hard drives require an IDE interface compatible with UltraATA/100 or 133 standards to achieve best performance. If you are installing the drive in a PC that does not support that specification on the motherboard, your choices are to accept lesser performance or to install an add-on IDE controller board that supports the desired standard.

1. Locate three different IDE controller boards online that will support an UltraATA/133 hard disk, and write the URLs where detailed specifications are available for each.

   http://_____

   http://_____

   http://_____

2. Given the price and features of each of the above, which is the best value, and why?

   _____

   _____

   _____

   _____

   _____

3. Look in the USENET newsgroups (for example, from http://groups.google.com) for customer opinions about the IDE controller board you chose in step 2. Write down your findings, including any problems or limitations that consumers have reported.

_____

_____

_____

_____

_____

4. Find a Web site where you can download BIOS and/or Windows driver updates for the controller card you chose in step 2, and write its URL below.

http://_____

5. On the Web, find the largest capacity IDE hard drive currently available from Seagate.

a. What is its capacity? _____

b. Will this drive work with the controller you chose in step 2? If not, why?

_____

_____

_____

_____

12 Performing Disk Management Tasks

Disks and disk drives are considered hardware, but when you interact with them, you must do so through the operating system. For example, you must format floppy disks before use, and you must partition and format hard disks. Once a disk has been properly formatted and has had data stored on it, you can view and edit its content through the operating system, too. These projects provide an opportunity for you to practice these skills.

Project 12A: Write-Protecting a Floppy Disk

Time to Complete: 5 minutes
Needed: A working Windows PC; a 3.5-inch floppy disk
Optional: A 5.25-inch floppy disk and drive
Reference: Page 423 of the textbook

1. From Windows or from a command prompt, copy a file to a 3.5-inch floppy disk.

2. Write-protect your 3.5-inch floppy disk by sliding the tab in its corner. When the disk is write-protected, should the tab be open or closed? _____

3. Reinsert the floppy disk in the drive, and try to delete from it the file that you placed there in step 1. What error message appears?

   _____

4. Remove write-protection from the floppy disk, and try again to delete the file. Are you now able to do it? _____

5. (Optional) If you have a 5.25-inch floppy disk and a 5.25-inch floppy drive, write-protect the disk by placing a sticker over the notch in its corner. Then try to copy a file to the disk from Windows or from a command prompt. What error message appears?

   _____

Project 12B: Formatting a Floppy Disk

Time to Complete: 5 minutes
Needed: A working Windows PC; a 3.5-inch floppy disk
Reference: Pages 424 through 427 of the textbook

1. Double-click the clock on the Windows taskbar, opening the Date and Time Properties dialog box. Keep the clock in this window on-screen so you can time the formatting process.

2   Insert a floppy disk. It should not contain any files you want to keep.

3. From the My Computer window in Windows, right-click the floppy drive and click Format.

4. Enter a label in the Volume Label text box (such as your last name or today's date).

5. Click Format and then click OK to confirm. Wait for the disk to be formatted. As it is formatting, watch the clock in the Date and Time Properties dialog box. How long did the formatting take? _____

6. A confirmation box appears when the formatting is complete; click OK.

7. Mark the Quick Format check box in the Format dialog box and then reformat the disk. Time it again; how long did it take this time? _____

Project 12C: Setting Up a Single-Partition Hard Disk

Time to Complete: 10 to 15 minutes
Needed: A working PC; a new hard disk (or one that contains files you do not want to keep); a Windows 9x startup floppy disk containing the FDISK and FORMAT utilities
Reference: Pages 428 through 437 of the textbook

1. Install the hard disk in the PC if it is not already installed, and make sure that BIOS Setup recognizes it. (See the Chapter 10 and Chapter 11 projects.) For this project, use a hard drive that contains nothing you want to keep, or use a new, unpartitioned drive.

2. Boot from the Windows 9x startup floppy disk.

3. Key **FDISK** and then press Enter to start the Fixed Disk Utility application, as shown here.

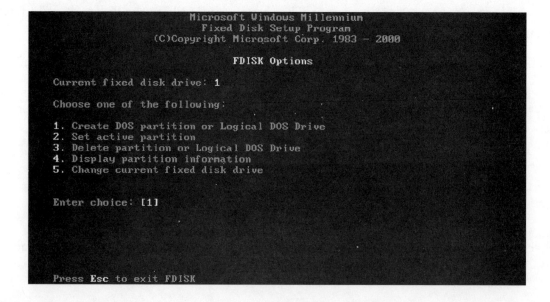

```
                    Microsoft Windows Millennium
                     Fixed Disk Setup Program
                (C)Copyright Microsoft Corp. 1983 - 2000

                         FDISK Options

Current fixed disk drive: 1

Choose one of the following:

    1. Create DOS partition or Logical DOS Drive
    2. Set active partition
    3. Delete partition or Logical DOS Drive
    4. Display partition information
    5. Change current fixed disk drive


Enter choice: [1]




Press Esc to exit FDISK
```

4. If there is more than one physical hard disk installed in this PC, make sure you are working with the one that you want. The first physical hard drive appears by default; use the Change Current Fixed Disk Drive command to change to another one if needed.

> ┌─ C A U T I O N ───
> │
> │ Be very certain you have chosen the correct physical drive before you delete any partitions. After changing to a
> │ different drive in step 4, use the Display Partition Information command to confirm that the drive is the one you
> │ think it is.
> │

5. If there are any existing partitions, delete them.

6. Create a primary partition that occupies all the available space. The utility will automatically set it as the active partition.

7. Press Esc to exit the utility. Restart the computer (again using the startup floppy) so that a drive letter can be assigned to the new partition.

8. Format the new partition using the FORMAT command at the command prompt.

Project 12D: Setting Up a Multi-Partition Hard Disk

Time to Complete: 10 to 15 minutes
Needed: A working PC; a new hard disk (or one that contains files you do not want to keep); a Windows 9x startup floppy disk containing the FDISK utility
Reference: Pages 428 through 437 of the textbook

1. If possible, complete Project 12C first, so that the drive is already physically installed in the PC and you already have some experience setting up a single-partition drive.

2. Boot from the Windows 9x startup floppy disk.

3. Key **FDISK** and then press Enter to start the Fixed Disk Utility application.

4. If there is more than one physical hard disk installed in this PC, make sure you are working with the one that you want. The first physical hard drive appears by default; use the Change Current Fixed Disk Drive command to change to another one if needed.

5. Delete any existing partitions. If you completed Project 12C, you will have a single primary partition to delete.

6. Create a primary partition that occupies approximately one-third of the total space on the drive.

7. Create an extended partition that occupies the remaining space on the drive.

8. Create two logical drives on the extended partition, each of which occupies half of the extended partition.

9. Press Esc to exit the utility and then restart the computer so that drive letters can be assigned.

10. Format each of the new drive letters using the FORMAT command at the command prompt.

Project 12E: Examining Disk Properties

Time to Complete: 10 minutes
Needed: A working PC with Windows 9x/Me, 2000, or XP
Reference: Pages 443 through 449 of the textbook

1. Open My Computer, right-click a hard disk, and then choose Properties. On the General tab, gather the following information.

   File system: _____

   Used space: _____

   Free space: _____

   Capacity: _____

2. What is the current volume label (name) assigned to this disk, if any?

   _____

3. Change the volume label to your last name.

4. Open the System Information utility (Start/Programs/Accessories/System Tools/System Information).

5. In the left pane, double-click Components, double-click Storage, and then click Drives.

> **NOTE**
>
> In System Information, a "drive" is considered a logical drive letter, while a "disk" is considered a physical hard disk drive. The same is true for Computer Management, which you will work with in step 10.

6. What additional information do you get about your drive using System Information that you did not get by viewing its properties in step 1?

   _____

7. Click Disks in the left pane. Information about the physical disk drive appears. List at least five things you learned about the disk by reading this information.

   _____

   _____

   _____

   _____

   _____

8. In the left pane, click IDE. Information about the IDE interface to the drives appears.

   a. How many IDE interfaces does your PC have? _____

   b. What IRQs do they use? _____

9. Close the System Information window.

10. If you are using Windows 2000 or XP, do the following (otherwise the project is complete).

    a. Open Computer Management. To do so, from the Control Panel, double-click Administrative Tools and then double-click Computer Management.

    b. In the left pane, click Disk Management.

    c. In the top right pane, how many drives (also called volumes or partitions) are listed? _____

    d. Do all of them report a status of Healthy? If not, what is the status of the non-healthy one(s)?

       _____

    e. Which drive letter represents the system partition? _____

    f. Which drive letter represents the boot partition? _____

    g. Which drive letter contains the paging file? _____

    h. In the bottom right pane, how many hard disks are listed? _____

       How many CD drives? _____

    i. Right-click on the name Disk 0 in the bottom right pane and then choose Properties. Are these the properties for the whole physical disk or for an individual partition?

       _____

    j. Click Cancel to close the Properties box.

    k. Close the Computer Management window.

Project 12F: Managing Disks on Remote Computers

Time to Complete: 10 minutes
Needed: Two or more networked Windows 2000 or XP computers; Administrator-level access to both PCs

Disk Management is a very handy tool in Windows 2000 and XP, but it can be even handier when run through the Microsoft Management Console (MMC) because you can check the disks on other PCs in the network (provided you have the needed network permissions).

1. Make sure that you have Administrator-level access to both PCs through the network. Ask your instructor or a network administrator to help set this up (or just try it if you are not sure). You will learn more about network permissions later in the course.

2. Choose Start and then Run. Key **MMC** and then click OK. This opens the Microsoft Management Console.

3. Choose File and then Add/Remove Snap-in. Click the Add button in the dialog box that appears.

4. Click Disk Management on the list of services in the Add Standalone Snap-in dialog box and then click Add to add it to the console.

5. At the Disk Management dialog box, click the option button for The following computer, key the network share name of the PC to which you want to refer, and then click Finish (see example below).

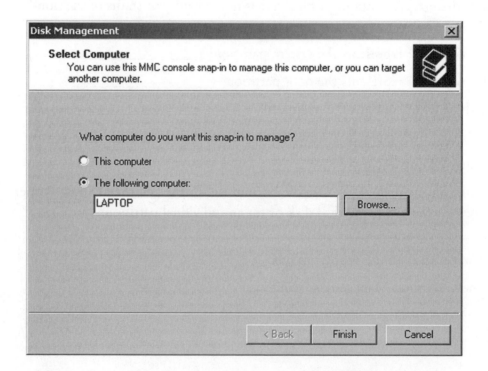

6. Click Close to close the Add Standalone Snap-in dialog box and then click OK to close the Add/Remove Snap-in dialog box.

7. In the right pane, double-click Disk Management. If you have the needed permissions for the remote PC, Disk Management displays its disks, the same as it did for your own local disks in Project 12E. If an error message appears, you lack the necessary permissions. You can choose to troubleshoot the permissions now, or wait until later chapters when you have learned more about Windows networking.

8. To save this console for later use, choose File and then Save. Key a name for the saved console in the Name box and then click OK. You can later reopen this console from the File/Open command in Microsoft Management Console.

9. Close the MMC window.

13 Managing CD Drives

CD drives are as commonplace as floppy drives these days. You are likely to encounter many different types, including CD-ROM, CD-R, CD-RW, DVD, and others. They all physically install the same way, however, and they all can function as normal CD-ROM readers. In these projects you will practice installing and configuring CD drives, and making your own CDs with a CD-R or CD-RW drive.

Project 13A: Installing an IDE CD Drive

Time to Complete: 10 to 20 minutes
Needed: A PC with at least one free 5.25-inch (large) drive bay and at least one free IDE position; a CD drive (any type)
Optional: A sound card; a CD audio cable
Reference: Pages 465 through 467 of the textbook

1. Examine the existing IDE devices installed in your PC, and list them here.

   Primary master: _____

   Primary slave: _____

   Secondary master: _____

   Secondary slave: _____

2. Determine the optimal position for the new CD drive, keeping in mind that the best configuration may involve moving some of the existing IDE devices. List the new configuration here.

   Primary master: _____

   Primary slave: _____

   Secondary master: _____

   Secondary slave: _____

3. Explain the factors that went into your decision-making in step 2.

   _____

   _____

   _____

   _____

   _____

   _____

4. If any of the existing IDE devices need to change position, change them now, including changing any jumper settings if needed. Describe what you did below.

_____

_____

_____

_____

_____

_____

5. Prepare a bay to accept the new CD drive, and install it there. Connect it to the motherboard and the power supply via ribbon cable and power cable, respectively. With which other IDE device, if any, does this new CD drive share a ribbon cable?

_____

6. (Optional) If the PC has a sound card, connect the sound card to the CD drive with an audio cable.

7. Replace the cover on the PC, and start it up. Watch the screen to see whether there is any indication that the BIOS Setup program recognizes the new drive.

8. In Windows, check the My Computer window for the new drive. If it does not appear there, troubleshoot the problem, and explain your troubleshooting process below.

_____

_____

_____

_____

_____

_____

Project 13B: Enabling CD Support from a Windows 98 Startup Disk

Time to Complete: 5 minutes
Needed: A working PC with a CD drive; a Windows 98 or Windows Me startup floppy
Reference: Pages 468 through 470 of the textbook

Windows 95 and higher supports CD drives automatically through the graphical user interface (GUI), so you do not need to worry about a driver for your CD drive. When you boot from a startup floppy, however, you can choose whether or not to install a real-mode driver for the CD drive, depending on whether you will need to access the CD drive during that session. Windows 98 and Windows Me place a variety of real-mode CD drivers on their startup floppies, and when you boot from such a floppy and choose to enable CD support, it attempts to load a compatible driver.

N O T E

If you do not have a startup floppy, make one from the Add/Remove Programs utility in the Control Panel.

---

1. Place the startup floppy disk in the floppy drive and then turn on the PC.

2. At the Startup menu, shown below, key **1** to select Start computer with CD-ROM support.

```
Microsoft Windows 98 Startup Menu

1. Start computer with CD-ROM support.
2. Start computer without CD-ROM support.
3. View the Help file.

Enter a choice: 1          Time remaining: 18




F5=Safe mode   Shift+F5=Command prompt   Shift+F8=Step-by-step confirmation [N]
```

3. Wait for the CD drivers to be loaded and a command prompt to appear. Watch the screen during the loading process to find out the CD drive's letter designation. What drive letter has been assigned to the CD drive? _____

---

4. At the command prompt, key the drive letter and a colon and then press Enter. The prompt changes to reflect that drive's name (for example, E:\>).

5. Place a CD in the drive and then key **DIR** at the prompt. A list of the CD's contents appears. List three files or folders that appear on the CD.

_____

_____

_____

Project 13C: Writing to CD-R and CD-RW Discs

Time to Complete: 10 to 30 minutes
Needed: A working PC with a CD-R or CD-RW drive; three blank CD-R discs; one blank CD-RW disc
Optional: Windows XP; Windows Media Player 8 or higher; several MP3 or WMF audio files
Reference: Pages 476 through 481 of the textbook

Do as many of these mini-projects as possible with your current equipment.

1. If you have Windows XP, complete the following steps.
   a. Insert a blank CD-R disc in the CD drive.
   b. In Windows Explorer, select several files that you want to store on a CD.
   c. Right-click the files, point to Send To, and then click CD Drive.
   d. Display the CD drive's content in Windows Explorer. Notice that the files appear with dimmed icons, indicating they are ready to be copied, as shown below.
   e. At this point, what must you do to write the files to CD, and what happens next?

_____

_____

_____

_____

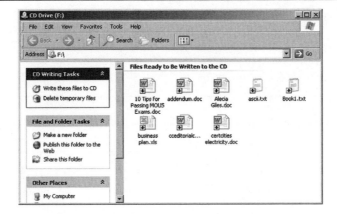

2. If you have a CD-RW drive with packet-writing software (such as DirectCD), complete the following steps.

    a. Insert a CD-RW disc (not a CD-R) in the CD drive.

    b. In Windows Explorer, select several files that you want to store on a CD.

    c. Drag and drop the files to the CD drive in the folder tree.

    d. Approximately how long did it take to write the files? _____

    e. Select additional files, and copy them to the CD-RW disc as well.

    f. Delete the files from the CD-RW that you copied there in step c.

    g. Given that you can write and delete freely from a CD-RW disc, why do you think CD-RW discs are not used as a substitute for a hard disk?

_____

_____

_____

_____

3. If you have Windows Media Player 8 or higher and some WMF or MP3 format audio clips (i.e., songs), complete the following steps.

    a. Insert a blank CD-R disc in the CD drive.

    b. Open Windows Media Player.

    c. Create a Playlist containing the files you want to record to CD, and display the playlist.

    d. Click the Copy to CD or Device button.

    e. Clear the check box next to any tracks that you do not want to be recorded to CD, as shown on page 99.

    f. Click the Copy Music button.

    g. How many tracks fit on your CD? _____
How many megabytes do they occupy? _____

4. Play your new CD in Windows Media Player. Did it appear to record all tracks correctly? Document any problems you notice.

_____

_____

_____

5. If you have a third-party CD burning application, complete the following steps.

   a. Insert a blank CD-R disc in the CD drive.

   b. Use your CD burning software to create a backup of your important data files. Document the steps you followed.

   _____

   _____

   _____

   _____

   _____

   _____

Project 13D: Adding CD Support to a Windows 95 Startup Disk

Time to Complete: 10 to 15 minutes
Needed: A working PC with a CD drive; a Windows 95 startup floppy; a real-mode driver file for the CD drive; MSCDEX.EXE.
Reference: Pages 470 through 471 of the textbook

Windows 95 does not place real-mode CD drivers on its startup floppy, unlike 98 and Me. Therefore, if you want CD access from a command prompt after booting from a Windows 95 startup disk, you must manually edit the disk's content and startup files.

┌─ **N O T E** ──
│
│ If you do not have a startup floppy, make one from the Add/Remove Programs utility in the Control Panel.
│
└──

1. In Windows 95, copy the file MSCDEX.EXE to the startup floppy. It is located in C:\Windows\Command. In MS-DOS, copy the file MSCDEX.EXE to the startup floppy. It is located in C:\Dos.

┌─ **N O T E** ──
│
│ If MSCDEX.EXE is not in the expected location, use the Find command in Windows 95 to locate it.
│
└──

2. Locate a real-mode driver for the CD drive, and copy it to the startup floppy. It may be on a floppy disk that came with the CD drive, or it may be in a folder on a hard drive. Make a note of the file name.

3. Open the CONFIG.SYS file from the startup floppy in a text editing program (Notepad in Windows or EDIT in MS-DOS), and add the following line to the bottom of the file:

DEVICE=A:*file* /D:*name*

You can use any name you want for the *name*. For example, if the CD driver file is called SSCDROM.SYS, and you wanted to use SSCD000 for the name, the line you add would be:

DEVICE=A:\SSCDROM.SYS /D:SSCD000

4. Save your changes to CONFIG.SYS, and open the AUTOEXEC.BAT file from your startup CD in the text editor program.

5. Add the following line to the bottom of the file:

   A:\MSCDEX.EXE /D:*name*

   Use the same name that you used in step 3. For example:

   A:\MSCDEX.EXE /D:SSCD000

6. Save your changes and exit the text editor program.

7. Exit Windows and boot from the startup floppy.

8. Wait for the CD drivers to be loaded and a command prompt to appear. Watch the screen during the loading process to find out the CD drive's letter designation. What drive letter has been assigned to the CD drive? _____

9. At the command prompt, key the drive letter and a colon and then press Enter. The prompt changes to reflect that drive's name (for example, E:\>).

10. Place a CD in the drive, and then key **DIR** at the prompt. A list of the CD's contents appears. List three files or folders that appear on the CD.

   _____

   _____

   _____

Project 13E: Creating a Bootable CD

Time to Complete: 10 minutes
Needed: A working Windows PC with a CD-R or CD-RW drive; CD burning software (such as Roxio Easy CD Creator); a startup floppy for Windows 95, 98, or Me
Reference: Pages 481 through 482 of the textbook

1. What CD burning application do you have? _____

2. Insert a blank CD-R in the CD writer, and insert your Windows 9x startup floppy in the floppy drive.

3. Start the CD burning application, and create a bootable CD that emulates the startup floppy. The steps are different depending on your software; document the steps below.

_____

_____

_____

_____

_____

_____

4. Restart the PC, and enter the BIOS Setup program. Set it to prefer the CD over the hard disk as a boot device. Document the steps for doing so.

_____

_____

_____

_____

5. Remove the floppy disk from the drive, but leave the CD. Restart the PC, and let the PC attempt to boot from the CD. If it is not successful, troubleshoot and document your steps.

_____

_____

_____

_____

PART 4

Input and Output Devices

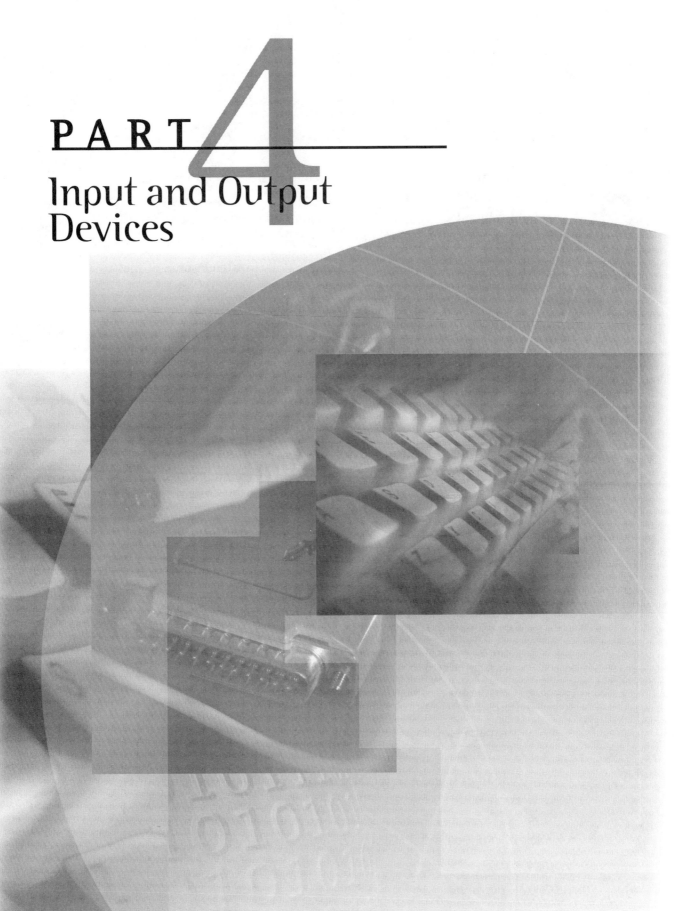

Although the PC's processing subsystem is critical, the systems that move data into and out of the PC are equally important. After all, who would want a PC that could process data at the highest speeds if there was no way to get data into or out of it?

In this part of the book you will practice skills involving some of the most common components for moving content into and out of a PC. Some of the skills you will demonstrate include:

- Replacing a video card
- Updating a video card driver
- Adjusting video card settings in Windows
- Troubleshooting display problems with games
- Installing a monitor INF file
- Changing the display refresh rate
- Using multiple video cards and monitors in the same PC
- Adjusting keyboard and mouse settings
- Setting up keyboard and mouse options for people with disabilities
- Setting up and configuring printers
- Installing a printer driver for a network printer

- Changing a toner cartridge
- Cleaning and aligning ink jets
- Controlling a print queue
- Scanning a photograph
- Transferring pictures to a PC from a digital camera
- Editing an image
- Choosing system sounds
- Installing a sound card and speakers
- Working with PC cards
- Setting up power management options
- Connecting external peripherals to a notebook PC
- Working with hardware profiles
- Installing RAM in a notebook PC
- Replacing a notebook PC's hard disk

Since end users spend most of their time working with input and output devices, these are devices that PC technicians are often called upon to support. Knowing how to make data entry and collection accessible for all levels of end users will make you very valuable to your clients.

14 Configuring Devices in Windows

Hardware interacts with the operating system through files called device drivers. Having the correct driver for a device is critical, as is having it installed properly under a compatible OS version. Plug-and-Play in Windows greatly simplifies the process of installing and configuring drivers, but problems do occasionally arise that a PC technician must be able to work through. These projects provide practice in working with device drivers in Windows.

Project 14A: Examining Device Resource Assignments in Device Manager

Time to Complete: 10 to 15 minutes
Needed: A working PC with Windows installed
Reference: Pages 498 through 506 of the textbook

1. Open Device Manager in Windows. The procedure is slightly different among Windows versions; write the steps you used.

   _____

   _____

   _____

2. Double-click the Ports category to see the COM and LPT ports on the list and then double-click the Printer Port (LPT1) to display its Properties box.

3. Click the Resources tab in the Printer Port (LPT1) Properties box. Based on the information shown, what resources does this port use?

   _____

4. Close the Properties box for the printer and then double-click Communications Port (COM1).

5. Click the Resources tab in the Properties box for COM1. Based on the information shown, what resources does this port use?

   _____

6. Close the Properties box for COM1.

7. If a device driver had a problem, what symbol would likely appear next to its icon?

   _____

8. If any device driver appears to have a problem, double-click it and look in its Properties box for information about what is wrong. Record your findings.

_____

_____

_____

_____

_____

9. If you are using Windows 2000 or XP, complete the following.

   a. Choose View and then Resources by Type.

   b. Click the plus sign next to Interrupt Request (IRQ).

   c. What IRQs (0 through 16) are not being used by any device?

   _____

   _____

   d. What IRQs are shared by more than one device? _____

   _____

   ┌─ N O T E ──┐
   │   │
   │ Remember, no devices will use IRQ2 because it is a cascade to IRQ9. It is not available for use, even though no │
   │ devices are using it.   │
   └──┘

10. If you are using Windows 9x or Me, complete the following.

    a. Double-click Computer at the top of the tree. The Computer Properties box opens.

    b. Click Interrupt Request (IRQ).

    c. What IRQs (0 through 16) are not in use? _____

    _____

    d. What IRQs are shared by more than one device? _____

    _____

11. Print a System Summary report by completing the following steps.
    - Using Windows 2000 or XP, click the Print button on the toolbar in Device Manager and then click Print.
    - Using Windows 9x/Me, click the Print button at the bottom of the Device Manager window, click System Summary, and then click OK.
12. List two pieces of information found on the System Summary report that you cannot find on-screen in Device Manager.

_____

_____

_____

Project 14B: Removing and Reinstalling a Device Driver

Time to Complete: 5 to 10 minutes
Needed: A working PC with Windows installed
Reference: Pages 507 through 514 of the textbook

Sometimes when a device is malfunctioning, removing and reinstalling its device driver can solve the problem.

1. Open Device Manager.

2. Locate the malfunctioning device. If no device is malfunctioning, choose a nonessential device such as a modem, NIC, LPT port, or COM port for practice.

   Which device will you choose for this exercise? _____

   C A U T I O N In step 2, do not choose a device for which you do not have a driver available. For example, if a modem is installed and you do not have the driver disk that came with it, do not choose that device for removal, because you might not be able to reinstall it correctly. You can often find the drivers you need on the Web, but availability is not certain.

3. Click the device and then press the Delete key on the keyboard. At the confirmation box, click OK.

4. Click the Refresh button to allow Windows to redetect the device and reinstall its driver.

5. If Windows does not automatically redetect the device, what are some possible reasons?

_____

_____

_____

_____

_____

_____

6. If Windows does not redetect the device, see Project 14E to reinstall it. If Windows *does* redetect the device, test it to make sure it is working. If it is not working, troubleshoot, and write the steps you took.

_____

_____

_____

_____

_____

_____

_____

Project 14C: Disabling a Device from Device Manager

Time to Complete: 5 minutes
Needed: A working PC with Windows 95 or higher installed
Reference: Pages 518 through 520 of the textbook

Disabling a device prevents it from using resources but does not remove its driver. This is useful if you need to disable a device, but you do not have the drivers available for a complete reinstall later.

1. Open Device Manager, and select the device to disable. For this exercise choose a noncritical device such as a modem or network card.

2. If you are using Windows 2000 or XP, choose Action and then Disable.

   If you are using Windows 9x/Me, complete the following.

   a. Click the Properties button.

   b. Mark the Disable in this Hardware Profile check box.

   c. Click OK.

3. How does the device now appear in Device Manager?

_____

4. Try using the device. What happens?

_____

5. Reenable the device and then try using it again. Does it work?

_____

Project 14D: Installing a Plug-and-Play Device

Time to Complete: 5 to 10 minutes
Needed: A working PC with Windows 95 or higher installed and a BIOS that supports Plug-and-Play; a PnP piece of hardware that is not currently installed in the PC (such as a circuit board)
Reference: Page 507 of the textbook

1. What is the type of device, the brand, and the model that you will be installing?

_____

2. Make sure you have a disk containing the drivers for the device you are installing. If you do not, download the drivers from the company's Web site, and have them ready on a disk or in a folder on your hard drive. If you downloaded drivers, write the URL where you got them.

http://_____

3. Shut down the PC, and physically install the new hardware in your PC.

4. Restart the PC.

5. Windows may detect the device and install a driver automatically, or it may prompt you for a driver. (Or it might not detect the new device at all.) Which happened for you?

_____

6. If you are prompted for a driver, click Cancel to avoid installing a driver now. You can install the driver this way, but it is better to run the Setup utility that came with the driver, if possible.

7. After Windows has finished starting up, run the Setup utility that came on disk or CD with the new device. Or, if you downloaded a driver or setup utility, run it from the folder on your hard disk where it is stored. What was the name and location of the Setup utility you ran?

_____

If you do not have a Setup utility for the device, but you do have a driver, do *one* of the following.

- Restart Windows so that it will redetect the new hardware and reprompt you for a driver. When prompted, point it to the location of the driver.
- Open Device Manager and then click Refresh to force Windows to redetect new hardware. When prompted, point it to the location of the driver.
- Open Device Manager and find the device on the list. It will probably have a yellow circle and exclamation point on it. Double-click it and then click the Driver tab. Click Update Driver, and follow the prompts to install the driver.

8. In Device Manager, confirm that the device's driver appears.

9. Double-click the device in Device Manager, and check that the device's status is "This device is working properly." If it is not, troubleshoot and then document your steps.

_____

_____

_____

_____

_____

_____

_____

_____

Project 14E: Installing a Non-Plug-and-Play Device

Time to Complete: 10 minutes
Needed: A working PC with Windows 95 or higher installed; a non-PnP device that is not already installed (such as a sound card, modem, or other circuit board)
Reference: Pages 507 through 508 of the textbook

If Windows does not detect a device, but it has detected other devices in the past, then the new device is broken, not installed correctly, or not a Plug-and-Play device. The exact steps for setting up a non-PnP device are different for each Windows version.

1. What is the type of device, the brand, and the model that you will be installing?

    _____

2. Make sure you have a disk containing the drivers for the device you are installing. If you do not, download the drivers from the company's Web site, and have them ready on a disk or in a folder on your hard drive. Write the URL for the Web site if you got the drivers on the Web.

    http://_____

3. Look in Device Manager to determine which IRQs and I/O addresses are free. Compare what is free to the available settings for the device (probably set with jumpers). Set up the device to use resources that are currently free. Write the settings you chose.

    _____

    _____

    _____

4. Shut down the PC and physically install the device.

5. Restart Windows.

6. Try running the Add New Hardware wizard from the Control Panel to see whether Windows can detect it. Sometimes Windows can detect non-PnP devices in a limited way.

> ┌─ N O T E ───
> │
> │ If the device is very old, it might not come with a Windows (protected-mode) driver. You can check the
> │ manufacturer's Web site to see whether a Windows driver is available. If not, you may need to allow the Setup
> │ software to modify the CONFIG.SYS and/or AUTOEXEC.BAT to add lines to load a real-mode driver for the device. This
> │ will allow it to work, but it might force Windows into a performance-degrading DOS Compatibility mode, so is not
> │ recommended except as a last resort.

7. Run the Setup program that came with the device (if you have it).

8. Check the device; is it working? If not, troubleshoot and then document your steps.

_____

_____

_____

_____

_____

Project 14F: Manually Changing a Device's Resource Assignments

Time to Complete: 5 to 10 minutes
Needed: A working PC with Windows 95 or higher installed (exercise works best with Windows 95 or 98)
Reference: Pages 514 through 518 of the textbook

This is a troubleshooting procedure for situations in which two or more devices have a conflict over a resource such as an IRQ or address.

1. Open Device Manager.

2. Are there any devices with conflicts? If so, explain.

_____

_____

_____

If not, choose a device that you will pretend has a conflict. A modem or sound card (ISA if possible) is a good choice for this exercise.

3. Double-click the device in Device Manager to open its Properties box.

4. On the Resources tab, if there is a Set Configuration Manually button, click it.

5. Clear the Use Automatic Settings check box.

> **N O T E**
>
> If the Use Automatic Settings check box is grayed out, you cannot manually change this device's resources; choose another device. If the device is involved in a conflict, choose the device with which it is conflicting.

6. Open the Setting Based On drop-down list and choose a different configuration. Try different configurations until you find one that resolves the conflict. Which configuration(s) worked?

    _____

7. If none of the configurations resolves the conflict, look in the Conflicting Device List to determine which resource is the problem. Write the conflict details here.

    _____

    _____

    _____

    Double-click that resource in the Resource Settings box to open a Properties box for that resource. Change the setting there if possible.

8. Continue resolving conflicts until no device conflicts remain. Explain what other conflicts you resolved and how you resolved them. If there were conflicts that you were not able to resolve, list them here, too.

    _____

    _____

    _____

    _____

    _____

    _____

    _____

    _____

    _____

Video Cards

The video card is the conduit between the monitor and the PC. Problems with a video card can result in no on-screen image at all, or in distortion or discoloration. Most of the time, however, problems with a video card are not with the hardware but with the card's Windows drivers. In these projects you will practice replacing a video card, updating its drivers, and adjusting its settings in Windows.

Project 15A: Replacing a Video Card

Time to Complete: 10 to 15 minutes
Needed: A working PC with a video card (*not* with video built into the motherboard)
Reference: Pages 545 through 547 of the textbook

1. Turn off the monitor and PC if either is on. Disconnect the monitor from your PC if it is connected.

2. Remove the cover from your PC, and locate the video card. How did you know that this was the video card?

   _____

3. Draw a picture of the monitor connector on the video card.

4. List the tools you will need to remove the video card and the safety precautions you should follow.

   _____

   _____

   _____

   _____

   _____

   _____

5. Remove the video card from its slot. Assuming the removed video card is still good, what handling precautions will you follow to prevent it from being damaged?

    _____

    _____

    _____

    _____

6. In what type of slot was the video card installed?

    _____

7. What information can you gather about this video card by reading the writing on the card itself or on the chips on the card?

    _____

    _____

    _____

    _____

8. Reinstall the video card in the same slot from which you removed it.

9. Replace the PC cover, and reconnect the monitor to the PC.

10. Turn on the PC and monitor and make sure that the video card is working. How can you tell if it is working?

    _____

    _____

    _____

11. If you run into any problems, troubleshoot them and then describe your actions.

    _____

    _____

    _____

    _____

Project 15B: Updating a Video Card Driver in Windows

Time to Complete: 10 to 20 minutes
Needed: A working PC; Web access
Reference: Pages 547 through 548 of the textbook

1. In Windows, display the Display Properties dialog box. (Right-click the desktop and then choose Properties.)

2. On the Settings tab, read the monitor and video card listed under Display. For example, in the figure shown, the monitor is Sony GDM-F500R and the video card is 32MB DDR NVIDIA GeForce2 GTS (Dell). Write your system's display devices here.

Monitor: _____

Video card: _____

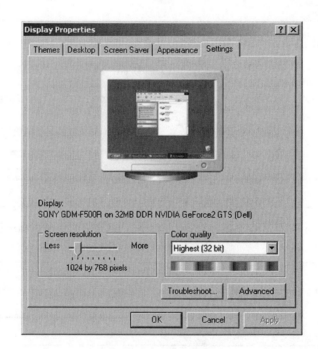

3. Find the version number and date of your current video card driver.

   Version number: _____

   Date: _____

   To find this information:

   • In Windows 2000/XP: From the Settings tab, click Advanced and then click the Adapter tab. Click the Properties button and then click the Driver tab.
   • In Windows 95/98/Me: From the Settings tab, click Advanced Properties and then click the Adapter tab. This will show you the version number, but the date is not visible from here. You can find the date by searching for the file names referenced under Current Files and checking the Date Modified in their properties.
   • In Windows NT 4.0: From the Settings tab, click Display Type. This will show you the version number. As with 95/98/Me, the date is not available, but you can find it by searching for the file names referenced under Current Files and checking their Date Modified.

4. On the Web, find a Web site from which you can download an updated driver for your video card for the exact operating system you have installed. Write the URL here.

   http://_____

   If you cannot find an exact match for your operating system, write the URL for the closest match you can find. Keep in mind that it is more important to exactly match the video card model than to exactly match the OS version, but that you need to stay in the same Windows family (e.g., a Windows 2000 driver will work for XP, but not for 98.)

5. What is the version number and date on the new driver?

   Version number: _____

   Date: _____

┌─ N O T E ──┐

   If the PC is a well-known brand, start looking for drivers at the PC maker's Web site. If the PC is an off-brand, but the video card is a well-known brand, look at the video card maker's site. If both are an off-brand, try a general search for the brand and model.

└──┘

6. If the new driver has a higher version number and a later date than your current driver, download and install it. Describe step-by-step the procedure for installing the new driver.

_____

_____

_____

_____

_____

_____

_____

_____

7. Restart Windows to confirm that the new driver works. If there are problems, troubleshoot them and then document your steps.

_____

_____

_____

_____

_____

_____

_____

NOTE

Some versions of Windows have a Roll Back Driver feature in the adapter's Properties box that can be used if installing a new driver causes display problems.

Project 15C: Adjusting Video Card Settings in Windows

Time to Complete: 10 to 20 minutes
Needed: A working PC
Reference: Pages 548 through 550 of the textbook

1. Which of these resolutions is your PC capable of, given its current video card, monitor, and Windows version? Circle as many as apply.

640x480	600x600	1024x768	1152x864
1280x1024	1600x1200	1792x1344	Others: _____

2. Which of these color depths is your PC capable of?

4-bit (16 color)	8-bit (256 color)	16-bit
24-bit	32-bit	Others: _____

3. Change your Windows display settings to the lowest combination of resolution and color depth that your PC supports. Write the settings you chose here.

   _____

4. Change your Windows display settings to the highest combination of resolution and color depth that your PC supports. Write the settings you chose here.

   _____

5. If the settings you chose in step 4 were not the highest settings you circled in steps 1 and 2, what is the limiting factor preventing that combination?

   _____

   _____

   _____

6. Change your Windows display settings to your preferred settings. These will vary depending on user preference; write the settings you chose here.

   _____

   _____

7. From the Display Properties, how do you access the Refresh Rate setting from your version of Windows?

   _____

   _____

8. Why is it important not to exceed the maximum refresh rate for your monitor for a particular resolution?

    _____

    _____

9. What is the maximum allowed refresh rate for your monitor for your current resolution, and how do you know this?

    _____

    _____

    _____

10. Set the refresh rate to the setting you specified in question 9.

Project 15D: Troubleshooting Display Problems with Games

Time to Complete: 5 to 10 minutes

Needed: A working PC with Windows; DXDIAG utility (included with Windows 98 and higher)

Reference: Page 551 of the textbook

DirectX is a suite of APIs through which games interact with the video and sound hardware. If a client is having a problem playing a game or running a program, the DirectX Diagnostic Utility (DXDIAG) can help in troubleshooting.

1. Choose Start and then Run. Key **DXDIAG** and then click OK.

2. Explore the utility, and run all the available tests that involve the display. (You may omit tests that are only for sound.) List the tests you performed and the results of each.

    _____

    _____

    _____

    _____

    _____

    _____

    _____

Sometimes the hardware acceleration for the video card can cause a problem with a game. One way to troubleshoot is to decrease the hardware acceleration used.

3. Find the settings for Hardware Acceleration. They are in different locations depending on the Windows version. Write the steps you took to locate them.

_____

_____

_____

4. Set the Hardware Acceleration setting to one setting lower than its current value. Restart the PC and then run a graphic-intensive program such as a game. Note any differences you experience.

_____

_____

_____

_____

_____

_____

_____

5. Restore the Hardware Acceleration to Full setting (or whatever value it was set to before step 4).

Monitors

Today's monitors can be either CRTs (Cathode Ray Tubes) or LCD (Liquid Crystal Displays). In Chapter 16 of the textbook, you learned the theory behind both of these monitor types; now you will have a chance to practice configuring them. Most high-quality monitors have many settings, and if a monitor's display is not perfect right out of the box, it can probably be improved by making some of the following adjustments.

N O T E

For best results, do these projects in the order in which they appear here because each depends on the previous ones. For example, you will not be able to accurately set the refresh rate without a monitor INF file installed, and you will not want to adjust the monitor until after you have set the refresh rate because different rates affect the appearance of the display differently.

Project 16A: Installing a Monitor INF File

Time to Complete: 5 to 15 minutes
Needed: A working PC in which the monitor has not yet been configured in Windows (that is, Windows reports the monitor as Unknown, or Standard Plug-and-Play Monitor, or some other generic specification)
Reference: Pages 572 through 573 of the textbook

1. Why does it matter that you install the correct INF file (driver) for your exact monitor model?

_____
_____
_____
_____

2. If you have a floppy disk that came with the monitor, locate it and have it ready. Otherwise, go to the monitor manufacturer's Web site and download a monitor INF file (driver file) for your exact brand of monitor. Write the URL where you found the file.

http://_____

3. Install the INF file for the monitor, either from the floppy disk or from your download. The steps are different in different Windows versions and different monitor models; write the steps you used here.

_____

_____

_____

_____

_____

_____

_____

_____

_____

Project 16B: Changing the Refresh Rate

Time to Complete: 5 to 15 minutes
Needed: A working PC with the correct INF file installed for the monitor
Reference: Pages 573 through 575 of the textbook

NOTE

You should set the refresh rate only after installing the monitor INF file (see Project 16A) to ensure that Windows has accurate information about the monitor's maximum refresh rate.

---

1. From the Display Properties, how do you access the Refresh Rate setting from your version of Windows?

_____

2. Why is it important not to exceed the maximum refresh rate for your monitor for a particular resolution?

_____

3. What is the maximum allowed refresh rate for your monitor for your current resolution, and how do you know this?

_____

_____

_____

4. Set the refresh rate to the setting you specified in step 3. Do you notice any difference in the display? If so, describe it.

_____

_____

_____

_____

_____

_____

_____

Project 16C: Adjusting Monitor Settings

Time to Complete: 5 to 15 minutes
Needed: A working PC; a monitor with an adjustable display
Reference: Pages 575 through 579 of the textbook

1. Some monitors have an on-screen display for adjusting the monitor, while others have a few simple knobs or thumbwheels. Describe the controls that your monitor has, their location, and how to access them.

_____

_____

_____

_____

2. If possible, degauss the monitor. Describe how you did it or explain why it is not possible on your monitor.

_____

_____

_____

_____

3. Move the display up, down, right, or left within the monitor frame so that it is centered on-screen. Describe how you did this.

_____

_____

_____

_____

4. Adjust the height and width of the display so that it exactly fills the monitor's viewable area. Describe how you did this.

_____

_____

_____

_____

5. If the display needs to be tilted, rotated, or otherwise adjusted so that the image is perfectly straight horizontally and vertically, do so, and explain how you did it.

_____

_____

_____

_____

6. Display a white screen in Windows, such as a word processing application, and look for convergence problems. How would convergence problems appear on a white screen?

_____

_____

_____

_____

7. Did you find any convergence problems? _____

8. Does your monitor allow you to fix convergence problems through its on-screen interface, or through knobs or wheels that are externally accessible? Describe how your monitor works.

_____

_____

_____

_____

9. Explain why you would not want to disassemble a monitor to adjust it.

_____

_____

_____

_____

Project 16D: Installing Multiple Video Cards and Monitors

Time to Complete: 10 to 15 minutes

Needed: A working PC with monitor; an extra PCI video card and an extra monitor; an operating system capable of supporting multiple monitors (such as Windows 2000 or XP)

Reference: Pages 570 through 572 of the textbook

1. Following all appropriate safety precautions, install a second video card in the PC, in a PCI slot. Describe the safety precautions you took while doing the installation.

_____

_____

_____

2. Connect a monitor to the second video card. You should now have two video cards and two monitors connected to the same PC. Turn on both monitors.

3. Start Windows, and in the Display Properties, set up the multiple monitors so that the Windows desktop is spread out over both of them. Describe step-by-step how you did it.

_____

_____

_____

_____

_____

_____

_____

4. If you were unable to set up the monitors together as a single Windows desktop, troubleshoot and describe the process below. Your troubleshooting might include researching on the Web to find out whether there are any known issues with certain brands of video cards. Include the URLs where you find useful troubleshooting information if applicable.

_____

_____

_____

_____

_____

_____

_____

Keyboards and Mice

Both of these common input devices are rather low-tech compared to some of the other parts of the PC, but they are very important to the end users who use them to interact with the PC. In these projects you will demonstrate that you know how to adjust keyboards and mice to fit user preferences and how to set them up to be more convenient for users with disabilities.

Project 17A: Identifying Keyboard Features

Time to Complete: 5 to 10 minutes
Needed: A keyboard (preferably a newer one)
Reference: Pages 589 through 595 of the textbook

1. How many keys does your keyboard have? _____

2. Draw pictures below of the symbols on the Windows-specific keys on a Windows keyboard, and label each drawing as to what each key does.

3. Is your keyboard a Windows keyboard? _____

4. Draw a picture below of an ergonomic keyboard, with labels showing what makes it ergonomic.

5. Is your keyboard an ergonomic keyboard? _____

6. Does your keyboard have any shortcut buttons for non-keyboard activities such as muting the system sound, adjusting the volume, controlling the CD audio player, or surfing the Web? If so, list them.

    _____

    _____

    _____

    _____

    _____

    _____

    _____

7. What type of connector does your keyboard use to connect to the PC: DIN, PS/2, or USB?

    _____

Project 17B: Adjusting Keyboard Settings in Windows

Time to Complete: 5 to 10 minutes
Needed: A working PC with Windows installed
Reference: Pages 599 through 600 of the textbook

1. Open the Keyboard Properties box from the Control Panel.

2. Set the Repeat Delay to its longest setting and then test it in the testing area of the dialog box.

3. Set the Repeat Delay to its shortest setting, and test it again. Based on your tests, describe what a repeat delay is.

   _____

   _____

   _____

4. Do the same tests as in steps 2 and 3, but for Repeat Rate. Based on your test, explain what repeat rate is.

   _____

   _____

   _____

5. Set the cursor blink rate to Fast and then click Apply.

6. With the Keyboard Properties window still open, open several different applications, and observe the insertion point/cursor in each of them. Based on your observations, does the Cursor Blink Rate setting pertain to all applications or just certain ones?

   _____

   _____

   _____

7. Switch back to the Keyboard Properties window, set the blink rate to a medium speed and then click OK.

Name: _____

Date: _____

Project 17C: Adjusting Mouse Settings in Windows

Time to Complete: 5 to 10 minutes
Needed: A working PC with Windows installed; a mouse
Reference: Pages 600 through 607 of the textbook

1. Open the Mouse Properties from the Control Panel.

> **NOTE**
>
> The exact options in the Mouse Properties depend on the Windows version and any special driver software installed.

2. Switch the mouse buttons so that the left button performs the right button's function and vice versa. The exact steps for doing this depend on the Windows version and the driver; describe how you did it.

   _____

   _____

   _____

3. Switch the buttons back to their original functionality.

4. Set the double-click speed to its slowest speed and then test it. Set it to its fastest speed and then test it again.

5. Set the double-click speed to a moderate rate and then test it. Adjust it as needed to suit your own preference.

6. If a novice user were having problems double-clicking because he could not click quickly enough, how would you adjust the double-click speed on his PC— faster or slower?

   _____

7. Change to a different pointer scheme. On which tab do you do this? _____

8. Give an example of a user who might benefit from using a different pointer scheme, and explain why.

   _____

   _____

   _____

9. Adjust the pointer speed to its fastest speed and then test it. Change it to its slowest speed and then test it again. Finally, set it to the speed you prefer for your own use.

10. List two other settings that you can adjust for your mouse, and explain what each one does and why it might be useful.

_____

_____

_____

_____

_____

_____

Project 17D: Using an On-Screen Keyboard

Time to Complete: 5 to 10 minutes
Needed: A working PC with Windows Me, 2000, or XP installed
Reference: Pages 607 through 608 of the textbook

Some users may not be able to use a keyboard because of a disability. For such users you can set up an on-screen keyboard so they can type by clicking the mouse.

> **NOTE**
>
> This utility can provide access for brief or emergency use, but for daily use the person will probably want a higher-end application.

1. Make sure that the Accessibility tools are installed. To check, choose Start, point to Programs, point to Accessories, and then point to Accessibility. If there is no Accessibility menu, the tools are not installed; install them with Add/Remove Programs. Were the tools already installed on your PC, or did you have to install them?

_____

2. Start the On-Screen Keyboard application. To do so, choose Start, point to Programs, point to Accessories, point to Accessibility, and then click On-Screen Keyboard.

3. For practice, open a Notepad window and key your full name and address using the On-Screen Keyboard.

4. Set the On-Screen Keyboard application to load automatically at startup. To do so, add a shortcut to it to the StartUp folder on the Programs menu.

5. Restart the PC, and confirm that the On-Screen Keyboard application loads automatically.

6. Turn off the On-Screen Keyboard, and remove its shortcut from the StartUp folder.

Project 17E: Moving the Mouse with the Keyboard Arrows

Time to Complete: 5 to 10 minutes
Needed: A working PC with Windows Me, 2000, or XP installed
Reference: Pages 608 through 609 of the textbook

Some users may have the opposite problem from the one described in Project 17D. They may be able to use a keyboard but unable to use a mouse. You can help such a user by setting up the arrow keys to move the mouse pointer. This feature is called MouseKeys.

1. Open the Control Panel and the Accessibility Options.

2. Turn on the MouseKeys feature. On which tab did you find it? _____

3. Click the Settings button for the MouseKeys feature, opening a Settings for MouseKeys dialog box.

4. Make a note of the shortcut key combination that turns on the MouseKeys feature. What is it?

   _____

5. List at least three other MouseKeys settings that are available in your version of Windows, and explain what each one does.

   _____

   _____

   _____

   _____

6. Close all open dialog boxes.

7. Does the MouseKeys icon appear in the notification area (next to the clock)? If not, turn it on using the shortcut key combination in step 4.

8. Experiment with moving the mouse pointer around on-screen using the arrow keys. Which set of arrow keys controls the mouse: the stand-alone set or the ones that are part of the numeric keypad?

   _____

9. Turn MouseKeys off. Explain how you did so.

   _____

Project 17F: Supporting Users with Disabilities

Time to Complete: 5 to 10 minutes
Reference: Pages 601 through 611 of the textbook

Depending on the Windows version, certain keyboard and mouse accessibility options and features may be available to help people with disabilities. Test your familiarity with these features in the following questions, looking up the answers in Windows as needed.

1. A user has a hard time holding down more than one key at a time. This makes it nearly impossible for to use shortcuts such as Ctrl + S for Save, for example. What feature could he use to make the Ctrl, Shift, and Alt keys function as a toggle?

   _____

2. A user cannot quickly release a key after pressing it, such that she often gets unintended repeated characters when typing. For example, when keying **test** she might get **ttteesssstttt**. What Windows feature could she use to help with this problem?

   _____

3. A user finds himself accidentally bumping the Caps Lock key, turning on the all-caps feature while typing. What feature could he use to help him notice when he has pressed that key?

   _____

4. A user cannot use a mouse, but she can type by tapping the keys on a keyboard with a stylus. What Windows accessibility features would assist her? Your answer will probably include more than one feature.

   _____

   _____

18 Working with Printers

If you work in a repair shop that is an authorized service center for a certain brand of printer, you will probably get lots of practice performing physical repairs on printers. Most PC technicians, however, will not be in this situation. The parts needed to physically repair a printer are usually specific to a certain brand and model, and can be difficult to get unless your company has a relationship with the manufacturer. However, that does not mean there is nothing you can do to help a user who is having trouble with a printer. Most of the time printer problems are actually driver problems or user errors, and almost any PC technician can deal handily with either of those issues without any special parts or equipment.

Project 18A: Connecting a New Printer

Time to Complete: 5 to 10 minutes
Needed: Any printer; a working PC running Windows 95 or higher; a cable suitable for connecting the printer to a PC
Reference: Pages 635 through 638 of the textbook

1. Which of these are possible interfaces for connecting a printer to a PC? Circle as many as apply.

   COM port   LPT port   IEEE 1394 (FireWire) port

   Universal Serial Bus (USB) IDE   SCSI

2. On the following figure, circle the port to which a parallel printer would attach.

3. With the printer and PC turned off, connect them. What type of cable did you use? Draw a picture below of the ends of the cable, and label which end went to the printer and which end went to the computer.

4. Turn on the printer. Describe the self-test that it goes through, including what lights flash, what lights stay on, how long it takes, and so on.

_____

_____

_____

_____

_____

_____

5. Turn on the computer. Does Windows attempt to detect the new printer? _____

   If Windows prompts you for a driver for the printer, click Cancel because we will be working with drivers in the next project.

6. Shut down the computer.

Project 18B: Installing a Local Printer Driver

Time to Complete: 5 to 15 minutes

Needed: A PC with a printer physically attached to it; a Setup CD that came with the printer or a driver for the printer or Web access

Reference: Pages 640 through 642 of the textbook

1. Make sure the printer is turned on and online and then turn on the PC. If the PC prompts you for the location of a driver for the printer, point it to the driver files, either on your hard disk or CD. Or, if you do not have any driver files yet for this printer, click Cancel. If applicable, what was the path you supplied to the driver files?

    _____

2. If you installed driver files in step 1, do a test print through the printer's Properties box to see if the printer is working.
    a. How did you access the printer's Properties box, and what did you click to get the test print?

    _____

    _____

    _____

    _____

    b. Did the test print successfully? _____

3. Explain why installing the driver for a printer as you did in step 1 might not be the best method in some cases.

    _____

    _____

    _____

    _____

    _____

4. If you have a Setup CD for the printer that contains drivers for your exact version of Windows, put it in the CD drive. Otherwise, go to the printer manufacturer's Web site and download a Setup utility for the printer for your OS version. If you downloaded a setup utility, write the URL for the Web site.

    http://_____

5. Run the Setup utility, and then test the printer again.

    a. Did the test print successfully? _____
    b. How, if at all, is the printer installed differently from the Setup utility than it was when you installed it by supplying the driver location in step 1?

    _____

    _____

    _____

    _____

6. Now suppose you want to update the printer's driver without removing and reinstalling it. Write the step-by-step procedure you would follow to do so.

_____

_____

_____

_____

_____

_____

_____

Project 18C: Installing a Network Printer Driver

Time to Complete: 5 to 15 minutes
Needed: A PC connected to a LAN on which there is at least one shared printer
Reference: Pages 640 through 642 of the textbook

1. Open the Printers dialog box (or Printers and Faxes) from the Control Panel or from the Start menu.

2. Double-click Add Printer (or Add a Printer) to start the Add Printer Wizard.

3. When asked whether you are installing a local or network printer, choose Network.

4. Browse for the printer when prompted for a path. Write the path here for the printer you chose.

   http://_____

5. Finish the Add Printer Wizard. The exact steps depend on your Windows version. Write the steps that you followed.

_____

_____

_____

_____

_____

_____

_____

_____

6. Do a test print. Did the test print successfully? _____

   If not, troubleshoot and then document your steps.

   _____

   _____

   _____

   _____

   _____

7. What issues might you encounter when trying to use a shared network printer installed on a client PC that runs a different operating system from yours, and how could you resolve them?

   _____

   _____

   _____

   _____

   _____

Project 18D: Cleaning and Aligning Ink Jets

Time to Complete: 5 to 15 minutes
Needed: An inkjet printer attached to a working Windows-based PC
Reference: Pages 655 through 656 of the textbook

1. What symptoms would an inkjet printer exhibit if one or more of its ink jets were clogged?

   _____

   _____

   _____

2. Locate the manual for the printer and find out how to clean the ink jets in stand-alone mode (that is, not relying on the PC). It is probably a matter of pressing certain buttons on the printer in a certain sequence. If you cannot locate a manual, find the information online. Clean the ink jets, and then write the instructions for doing so.

_____

_____

_____

3. Display the printer's Properties in Windows, and find a setting or button in that box that cleans the ink jets. What is the name of that button or setting, and on which tab did you find it?

_____

_____

_____

4. In the Properties dialog box for the printer, find a setting or button that prints a nozzle check, so you can see whether any of the jets are clogged. Print a nozzle check, and describe the results here. Do any of the nozzles appear to be clogged? How can you tell? Which colors appear to be clogged, and which appear to be working perfectly?

_____

_____

_____

_____

_____

5. If any nozzles were clogged, run the cleaning utility again, and then print another nozzle test pattern. Keep doing this until all nozzles are unclogged. How many repetitions of the cleaning/checking process did you go through? _____

6. What is the drawback to performing repeated cleanings?

_____

_____

_____

7. Look in the printer's Properties box for a utility that aligns the print head. If you find one, run it, and make any adjustments needed. Describe the process.

_____

_____

_____

_____

_____

8. What symptoms would an inkjet printer exhibit if its print head were out of alignment?

_____

_____

_____

_____

Project 18E: Changing a Toner Cartridge

Time to Complete: 5 to 15 minutes

Needed: A laser printer; a new toner cartridge kit for that printer

Reference: Pages 652 through 653 of the textbook

1. What symptoms would a laser printer exhibit if it needed to have the toner cartridge replaced?

_____

_____

_____

_____

2. Remove the toner cartridge from your printer. Describe how you did it.

_____

_____

_____

_____

_____

3. Some laser printers have the drum built into the toner cartridge; on others it is separate. Which is the case on your printer, and how can you tell?

_____

_____

_____

_____

4. Some toner cartridges have a corona wire in them that can be cleaned without disassembling the cartridge. Does yours have one of these? If so, what would you use to clean it?

_____

_____

_____

_____

5. Install the new toner cartridge in your printer. Describe any preparatory steps you took before inserting it. For example, did you remove any shipping tape from the cartridge?

_____

_____

_____

_____

6. Some printers have a strip of felt on a plastic bar that needs to be changed when the toner cartridge is changed. If your new toner cartridge came with one, that is a sign that your printer has this feature. If your printer has this, draw a picture of the printer below and draw an arrow pointing to the area where the felt strip is installed.

7. On some printers, you must run a cleaning utility after installing a new cartridge. Is this the case with your printer? If so, describe the procedure for running the utility.

_____

_____

_____

_____

8. From Windows, print a test page. If the test page does not look good, troubleshoot and then document your steps here.

_____

_____

_____

_____

Project 18F: Working with a Print Spool (Queue)

Time to Complete: 5 to 15 minutes
Needed: A laser printer; a new toner cartridge kit for that printer
Reference: Pages 657 through 659 of the textbook

1. Start with a working local printer in Windows. Print a test page if needed to confirm it is working.

2. Display the print queue for the printer. To do so, double-click the printer icon in the Printers folder (Control Panel).

3. Pause the print queue as a whole. What is the menu command for doing this?

_____

4. Open a text editing program, such as Word, and key a few sentences. Print the document with the printer you paused in step 3.

5. Key additional text and then print again.

6. Open a graphics program, such as Paint, and draw a few shapes; then print them to the same printer.

7. Open a spreadsheet program, such as Excel, and enter data into a few cells. Print it to the same printer.

8. Return to the print queue window. How many print jobs appear in the queue? _____

9. Pause the first two print jobs individually. What is the menu command for doing this?

_____

10. Right-click the third job and choose Properties. What options are available for setting the job's priority? The options will depend on the Windows version and the printer model.

   _____

   _____

   _____

   _____

   _____

   _____

11. If possible, set the priority for the third print job to be as high as possible. Setting the priority for the job may not be possible, depending on your system.

12. Un-pause the queue as a whole. Which print job prints next? _____

13. Delete the second paused job. How did you do this?

   _____

14. Un-pause the remaining paused job.

15. Close the print queue, and return to the Printers window (or Printers and Faxes).

16. Right-click the background in the Printers window and choose Server Properties (if available, depending on Windows version). If you are able to access it, list three things you can do in the Server Properties window.

   _____

   _____

   _____

   _____

19 Imaging and Sound Devices

As more and more end users start enjoying scanners, digital cameras, microphones, digital video cameras, and other input and output devices for sounds and images, the average PC technician will be called upon to support these devices. In these projects you will practice your own mastery of scanners, digital cameras, and sound input and output. You will also demonstrate how to configure the sound features of Windows for people with disabilities.

Project 19A: Scanning a Photograph

Time to Complete: 5 to 15 minutes
Needed: A PC; a scanner
Reference: Pages 683 through 684 of the textbook

1. What is the brand and model of your scanner, and what type of interface does it have?

    _____

    _____

    _____

2. If your scanner is not connected to the PC, and its software is not set up, do so to prepare it for use. Document the steps you took and any challenges you faced.

    _____

    _____

    _____

    _____

    _____

    _____

    _____

3. What version of Windows do you have? _____

4. Does this version of Windows include the Scanner and Camera Wizard? _____

5. Does your version support your scanner make and model? How can you determine this?

    _____

    _____

    _____

6. Place a photograph, magazine clipping, or other item on the scanner, and scan it. Describe the software you used for this and the steps you followed.

_____

_____

_____

_____

_____

_____

_____

7. Save the file, and call it MYSCAN. Use any file format that your software will support. What format did you use? _____

Project 19B: Transferring a Digital Camera Picture to Windows

Time to Complete: 10 to 15 minutes
Needed: A PC; a digital camera
Reference: Pages 692 through 695 of the textbook

1. What brand and model of digital camera do you have?

_____

2. What version of Windows do you have?

_____

3. Is your camera on the HCL for your version of Windows? _____

4. List the Web site where you found the answer to step 3.

http://_____

5. Explain how the answer to step 3 affects how you will interact with the camera under versions of Windows that include the Scanner and Camera Wizard.

    _____

    _____

    _____

    _____

    _____

6. Take several pictures with your camera. What medium does the camera use to store the pictures inside it?

    _____

7. Connect the camera to the PC. What type of connection did you use?

    _____

8. What are the advantages and disadvantages of the connection method you used as opposed to the connection methods that some other digital cameras might use?

    _____

    _____

    _____

    _____

9. Examine the pictures from the camera in Windows. What application are you using to do this? Is this your only choice on this PC? If not, what other applications could you use to browse the camera contents?

    _____

    _____

    _____

    _____

    _____

    _____

    _____

    _____

Name: _____

Date: _____

10. Pick two of the pictures from the camera, and transfer them to your hard disk. What are the default file names for the pictures?

_____

_____

11. Empty all of the pictures from the camera. How did you do this?

_____

_____

_____

_____

Project 19C: Image Editing

Time to Complete: 10 to 15 minutes
Needed: A PC with at least one graphics editing application installed
Reference: Pages 695 through 699 of the textbook

1. What graphics applications do you have installed in Windows?

_____

_____

_____

2. Select one of the graphics applications, and open one of the graphics from Project 19A or 19B in it. Or, if you did not do either project, open another saved graphic. Which file did you choose?

_____

3. Do as many of the following as your graphics application will allow. Place a check mark next to the ones you have completed, and an X next to the ones that cannot be done in your software.

_____ a. Crop the picture to show only the most important area of it

_____ b. Color-correct the picture to make it more realistic and attractive

_____ c. Rotate the picture 90 degrees

_____ d. Save the file under a different name

_____ e. Convert the graphic to grayscale

_____ f. Save the file as a different file type

4. Match the following situations to the preferred graphic file format for that usage.

_____ Still graphic on a Web page   a. TIF

_____ Full-color photo for professionally printed newsletter   b. JPG

_____ Windows wallpaper   c. BMP

5. Create a new graphic in your graphics application, and save it in at least three different file formats. Compare the file sizes in Windows Explorer. What are the file sizes of each copy?

TIF _____

BMP _____

JPG _____

Project 19D: Installing a Sound Card and Speakers

Time to Complete: 10 to 20 minutes
Needed: A PC with at least one PCI slot free; a PCI sound card; audio cable (optional); speakers
Reference: Pages 708 through 710, 718 of the textbook

1. What is the brand and model of your sound card?

_____

2. If you do not have a Setup disk or a driver disk for the sound card, download the needed drivers from the Web and write the URL below.

http://_____

3. What precautions should you follow while installing a sound card to avoid harm to yourself and damage to the PC components?

_____

_____

_____

_____

_____

4. Following all necessary precautions, remove the cover from your PC and then install the sound card.

5. (Optional) If there is a CD drive in the PC, attach an audio cable from the CD drive to the sound card. What is the purpose of this audio cable?

   _____

   _____

6. What color is the speaker connector on sound cards that are color-coded?

   _____

7. On the following figure, draw an arrow pointing to the port(s) into which you would plug external speakers.

8. Connect speakers to the sound card and then turn on the speakers.

9. Replace the cover on the PC, start Windows, and allow Windows to detect the sound card. If prompted for the drivers, point the utility to the location containing them.

10. If you are not sure whether the drivers are installed correctly and the sound card is working, how can you check? Provide at least two different ways.

    _____

    _____

    _____

    _____

    _____

    _____

    _____

11. Draw a diagram below showing how the speakers are connected to one another and to your PC.

Project 19E: Choosing System Sounds

Time to Complete: 5 to 10 minutes
Needed: A PC with sound card and speakers
Reference: Pages 720 through 722 of the textbook

1. What Windows version are you using? _____

2. Which Control Panel applet do you use to change the system sounds in this Windows version? Circle one.

   a. Sounds and Audio Devices

   b. Sounds

   c. Sounds and Multimedia

   d. Multimedia

3. On which tab do you choose sound schemes? _____

4. What are the available sound schemes installed?

    _____

    _____

    _____

    _____

    _____

5. Select one of the sound schemes, and then listen to several of the sounds by clicking the sound and then clicking the Play button. Adjust the volume if needed.

6. Change one of the sounds in the scheme to a different sound on the Sounds list.

7. Change one of the sounds in the scheme to a sound that is *not* on the Sounds list.

8. Save the scheme under a new name.

9. Suppose a user wanted to keep system sounds turned on as a whole, but does not like the "You've Got Mail" sound that plays when using AOL. Describe how you would turn off that particular sound.

    _____

    _____

    _____

    _____

    _____

20 Portable PCs

Notebook and handheld PCs are becoming more popular, and PC technicians are increasingly being called upon to support and service them. While major repairs must be performed at authorized service centers (where the technicians have special training on the specific components and access to replacement parts), a well-rounded PC technician should be able to find his or her way around such basic tasks as working with PC Cards, power management, and replacing simple-to-access components like RAM and hard disks.

Project 20A: Working with PC Cards

Time to Complete: 5 minutes
Needed: A notebook PC with PC Card slots; a PC Card; Web access
Reference: Pages 739 through 740, 748 through 749 of the textbook

1. Which of the following devices are available in PC Card form? Circle your answers. Use the Web to search for PC Card versions of the devices if you are not sure.

   Memory   CPU   Hard drive   Modem   Ethernet NIC

   Sound Card   CD-ROM   Floppy drive   Keyboard   Mouse

   SCSI adapter   Parallel port FireWire port

2. With Windows running, insert a PC Card device in your notebook PC. What messages, if any, appear on-screen? What sounds, if any, do you hear?

   _____

   _____

   _____

   _____

   _____

   _____

   _____

3. Stop the PC Card using Windows and then physically remove the card from the PC. Describe how you did both.

_____

_____

_____

_____

_____

_____

4. Why should you not remove the PC Card without stopping it first using Windows?

_____

_____

_____

_____

_____

5. Most PC Cards sold today are Type II. What physical characteristic distinguishes Type II from Types I and III?

_____

_____

_____

Project 20B: Using Fn Keys

Time to Complete: 5 to 10 minutes
Needed: A notebook PC with an Fn key
Reference: Page 738 of the textbook

1. Certain keys on a notebook PC, when pressed in conjunction with the Fn key, function as a numeric keypad. These keys type numbers like a standard numeric keypad when the Numlock is (circle one) on / off, or function as an arrow keypad when NumLock is (circle one) on / off.

Name: _____

Date: _____

2. Mark the keys below that correspond to the numeric keypad when used with Fn.

0 _____   5 _____   - (minus) _____

1 _____   6 _____   + (plus) _____

2 _____   7 _____   / (divide) _____

3 _____   8 _____   * (multiply) _____

4 _____   9 _____   . (decimal) _____

3. Write the Fn features of each function key on your notebook PC's keyboard, or write *NA* if a key has no special Fn functionality.

F1 _____   F5 _____   F9 _____

F2 _____   F6 _____   F10 _____

F3 _____   F7 _____   F11 _____

F4 _____   F8 _____   F12 _____

4. Open Calculator in Windows, and using only the Fn numeric keypad, perform the following calculations.

a. 39,234.222 + 2,877.3101 = _____

b. 5,857,775 / 827,122 = _____

c. 299 * 23 = _____

Project 20C: Setting Up Power Options

Time to Complete: 10 to 15 minutes
Needed: A notebook PC that supports APM or ACPI power management
Reference: Pages 751 through 760 of the textbook

1. To which power management standard does your notebook PC conform? How do you know?

_____

_____

_____

_____

_____

2. Describe the power management features built into the PC's BIOS.

_____

_____

_____

_____

_____

3. From what Control Panel applet do you access the power management features of Windows?

_____

4. For each of the following statements, write *H* next to the statement if it applies to Hibernation and *S* if it applies to Standby. Some statements may apply to both and some to neither.

_____ a. Keeps RAM powered up

_____ b. Copies contents of RAM to the hard disk

_____ c. Consumes a small amount of power

_____ d. Consumes no power at all, so can be maintained indefinitely

_____ e. May cause lockups or failure to resume due to conflicts with BIOS power management

_____ f. Can be set up to occur when you press the Power button on the PC

_____ g. Shuts down the hard disk

_____ h. Stops the CPU

_____ i. Blanks the display

_____ j. Available only on portable computers

5. Set up the PC to go into hibernation mode when you press the Power button, and then press it to place the PC into hibernation.

6. Wait about 10 seconds and then press the Power button again to wake up the PC. If it does not wake up correctly, troubleshoot and then document your steps.

_____

_____

_____

_____

_____

_____

_____

7. Set up the PC to go into Standby mode after 5 minutes of idle time when running on batteries, and then unplug it and allow it to run on batteries until Standby occurs.

8. Move the mouse or press a key to wake up the PC. If it does not wake up correctly, troubleshoot and then document your steps.

_____

_____

_____

_____

_____

_____

Project 20D: Using External Peripherals

Time to Complete: 10 to 15 minutes
Needed: A notebook PC
Reference: Pages 740 through 742 of the textbook

1. Shut down the PC if it is running, and connect an external monitor and keyboard.

2. Restart the PC. Does the display appear: a) on the notebook's LCD screen, b) on the external monitor, or c) on both? _____

3. Which key(s) can you press to change the selection of the monitor being used? Describe how you would switch among the three possible settings listed in step 2.

_____

_____

_____

_____

4. Which keyboard is active: a) the notebook keyboard only, b) the external keyboard only, or c) both?

_____

5. In Windows, check the Display Properties. Can you set up the two monitors to work together with the desktop spread out over them? If so, set this up, and describe the process below. If not, explain why.

    _____

    _____

    _____

    _____

    _____

    _____

    _____

6. Shut down Windows, and disconnect the external keyboard. Connect an external mouse.

7. Start up Windows. Which mouse functions: a) the built-in pointing device only, b) the external mouse only, or c) both? _____

8. List three other external devices you could connect to this PC, and to which ports you would connect them.

    _____

    _____

    _____

    _____

9. If there is a single PS/2 port on the notebook PC, how could you connect both an external keyboard and an external mouse at the same time? List at least two options.

    _____

    _____

    _____

    _____

Project 20E: Working with Hardware Profiles

Time to Complete: 10 to 20 minutes
Needed: Any working Windows PC
Reference: Pages 761 through 766 of the textbook

1. Describe at least two computing situations in which the ability to have multiple hardware profiles is useful.

   _____

   _____

   _____

   _____

   _____

   _____

2. Which icon in the Control Panel do you double-click to access the Hardware Profiles feature in your version of Windows? _____

3. Create a new hardware profile called Basics. Describe how you do this.

   _____

   _____

   _____

   _____

4. Describe how to disable (not remove) a hardware device in Device Manager in your Windows version.

   _____

   _____

   _____

   _____

5. Reboot into the Basics hardware profile and disable all nonessential hardware in the Basics profile. List below the devices you disabled.

_____

_____

_____

_____

_____

_____

6. Reboot into your original hardware profile (probably Profile 1) and check the devices from the list in step 5. Are all of them working (that is, not disabled)? _____

7. Which IRQs are unused in your original hardware profile?

_____

_____

_____

8. Reboot into the Basics hardware profile. Which IRQs are unused in the Basics hardware profile?

_____

_____

_____

9. Reboot into your original hardware profile, and delete the Basics profile.

Project 20F: Installing RAM in a Notebook PC

Time to Complete: 5 to 15 minutes
Needed: A notebook PC; a removable stick of RAM for the PC (installed or not); Web access
Reference: Page 767 of the textbook

1. What is the brand and model of your notebook PC? _____

2. On the Web, find instructions (if possible) for upgrading the memory on your brand and model of notebook PC. Write the URL here.

http://_____

3. Locate the RAM slot in the notebook PC. It may be behind a plastic panel on the bottom of the PC, or you might have to do some minor disassembly such as removing the battery and/or lifting up the keyboard. Describe how you did it.

_____

_____

_____

_____

_____

_____

4. Is there already a removable stick of RAM in the slot? _____

If so, remove and examine it (following proper ESD precautions). Draw a picture of it below.

5. What can you determine about this RAM by the writing on it?

_____

_____

_____

6. Find information on the Web about what type of RAM would work in this PC, and write the URL here.

http://_____

7. If you removed the RAM in step 4, replace it now. If not, and you have some suitable RAM available, install it now.

8. Reassemble the PC, and start it up to confirm that the RAM works. Troubleshoot if needed and then document your steps.

_____

_____

_____

_____

_____

_____

Project 20G: Replacing a Notebook PC Hard Disk

Time to Complete: 15 to 30 minutes
Needed: A notebook PC; (optional) a new hard disk for a notebook PC; Web access
Reference: Pages 768 through 769 of the textbook

1. What is the brand and model of your notebook PC? _____

2. On the Web, look for instructions for replacing the hard disk on your brand and model of notebook PC. Write the URL here.

   http://_____

3. Determine what type of screwdriver(s) you need to access the hard disk. (Many notebook PCs use nonstandard screws such as T-8 Torx, for example.)

   _____

4. With the PC off and unplugged, remove the battery. Describe how you removed it (from which side of the computer it is accessed, whether you used a tool to remove it, and so on).

   _____

   _____

   _____

   _____

   _____

5. Disassemble the notebook PC enough to access the hard disk. Trace the ribbon cable from the motherboard (or some unexposed area of the system) to the hard disk. What differentiates this ribbon cable from the normal ribbon cable used inside a desktop PC?

_____

_____

_____

_____

_____

_____

6. Carefully disconnect the ribbon cable and power supply from the hard drive. There may be a plastic loop attached to the connector to help you unplug it, as shown below. Remove the screws holding it in place and lift it out.

7. Examine the removed hard disk. How is it different from the hard disk in a desktop PC?

_____

_____

_____

_____

8. Install the new hard disk, if you have one, or reinstall the old one. Document any problems you encountered.

_____

_____

_____

9. Reassemble the PC completely and then test it to make sure it works. If you installed a new hard disk you will need to partition and format it; do this if required.

PART 5

Networks, Modems, and the Internet

Computers have become increasingly interconnected in recent years, to the point where a stand-alone PC is actually a rarity. Almost every PC has at least a dial-up connection to the Internet, and many homes have their own small peer-to-peer networks as well. And of course, corporate large-scale networking is also alive and well.

In this section's projects, you will practice setting up and configuring devices that allow PCs to communicate with one another, including modems, networking hardware, and Internet connectivity devices such as DSL and cable terminal adapters. Some of the skills you will demonstrate include:

- Choosing network topologies and hardware
- Creating a peer-to-peer network
- Installing communications protocols in Windows Networking
- Sharing folders and printers
- Browsing shared resources on a LAN
- Mapping a network drive
- Working with network sharing permission settings
- Installing modems
- Testing and configuring modems
- Using a Terminal application
- Creating new Dial-Up Networking (DUN) connections
- Configuring an e-mail account
- Configuring a Web browser
- Working with Web security and privacy settings
- Using a Web content filter

As the Internet and networking become more and more a daily part of the average end user's experience, you can plan on fielding numerous questions about Internet usage and spending more of your on-the-job day supporting and troubleshooting network usage.

21 Networking Hardware Concepts

A basic knowledge of networking hardware is essential for a PC technician, since almost every computer these days is connected to some type of network. The Internet is the largest, best-known network, but corporate and home local-area networks (LANs) are also very common. In these projects you will demonstrate your ability to identify and select networking hardware and to install a Network Interface Card (NIC).

Project 21A: Identifying Networking Hardware

Time to Complete: 5 to 15 minutes
Needed: An ISA, PCI, or PC Card NIC
Reference: Pages 819 through 826 of the textbook

1. Indicate which of the following pictures shows an Ethernet 10/100BaseT NIC. _____

a.

b.

c.

d.

e

2. Which of the following cables would be appropriate for use in a 10/100BaseT network? Insert the appropriate letter(s). _____

a.

b.

c.

d.

e

f.

g.

h.

3. How is a NIC visibly different from an internal modem? List two ways.

_____

_____

4. With what network type is your NIC designed to work? For example, is it 10Base2? 10BaseT? 10Base5? Token Ring?

_____

_____

5. Write down the identifying information from your NIC, including brand, model, serial number, or other facts you can gather visually.

_____

_____

_____

_____

_____

6. On the Web, locate the manufacturer's Web site.

http://_____

7. Based on the specifications provided on the Web site for your model, list two features it has that were not evident from a visual examination.

_____

_____

_____

8. For which operating systems are drivers available for your NIC?

_____

_____

_____

9. Download the latest driver set for your PC's operating system, and store it on a floppy disk or in a folder on the hard disk that you create for this purpose. You will use these drivers in Project 21C, "Installing a NIC."

Project 21B: Identifying Networking Topologies

Time to Complete: 5 to 15 minutes
Reference: Pages 800 through 807 of the textbook

1. On the figures below, draw lines showing the physical connections involved in the specified topology.

Star topology:

Hub

Ring topology:

Hub

Bus topology:

Hub

2. Write the appropriate letter next to each of the following statements about physical topologies (A for Bus, B for Star, C for Ring, D for Mesh).

_____ a. Must be terminated on each end of the physical chain

_____ b. A group of PCs connects to a central gathering point

_____ c. The physical arrangement of an Ethernet 10Base2 workgroup

_____ d. The physical arrangement of an Ethernet 100BaseT workgroup

_____ e. Provides redundancy to ensure data can always reach its destination

_____ f. Requires a hub, MAU, or other connecting device

3. On the following figure, use a highlighter (or a pen with ink other than black) to trace the logical route that data would take from PC1 to PC3 in a network that uses a logical ring topology, such as Token Ring.

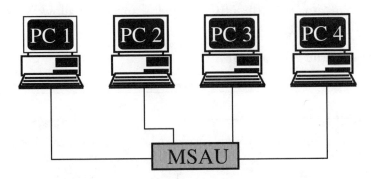

Project 21C: Installing a NIC

Time to Complete: 5 to 15 minutes
Needed: An ISA or PCI NIC; a PC with an available expansion slot
Reference: Pages 819 through 821 of the textbook

1. What safety precautions should you observe when installing a NIC?

_____

_____

_____

_____

_____

2. Observing the precautions you listed in step 1, remove the cover from the PC and identify the slot into which you will install the NIC. Is it PCI or ISA? _____

3. What would be the advantages of a PCI NIC over an ISA NIC?

    _____

    _____

4. If there is a backplate cover installed for that slot, remove it, and then insert the NIC in the slot. Secure it with a screw.

5. Replace the cover on the PC and start Windows.

    a. Does Windows detect the new NIC? _____

    b. Does it prompt you for a driver, or does it install the driver automatically? _____

6. If prompted for a driver, point the wizard to the location of the driver you downloaded in Project 21A. If you did not do this project, use the disk that came with the NIC, or click Cancel and allow Windows to finish loading, and then use the Web to find a driver.

7. Check Device Manager. In which category does the NIC appear?

    _____

    _____

8. Are any problems reported with the NIC in its Properties through Device Manager? If so, troubleshoot and then document your process.

    _____

    _____

    _____

    _____

    _____

    _____

    _____

    _____

Project 21D: Shopping for Wireless Ethernet Hardware

Time to Complete: 10 to 20 minutes

Needed: Web access

Reference: Pages 811 through 812, 826 through 827 of the textbook

1. On the Web, find the specifications (including speed and range) for the IEEE 802.11a wireless networking standard and write them below.

   _____

   _____

   _____

   _____

   _____

2. How is 802.11a different from 802.11b?

   _____

   _____

   _____

3. Suppose a client wants to install a small wireless network in his home. He has two desktop PCs and one notebook PC, and he wants to share a DSL Internet connection between them. Describe the hardware he would need to buy.

   _____

   _____

   _____

   _____

4. Research brands and models of the needed hardware by visiting consumer review sites. Make a recommendation of the exact brands and models of items to purchase.

_____

_____

_____

_____

_____

_____

5. Find at least two online stores where you can buy the brands and models you recommend in step 4. For each item listed above, specify where you would buy it (the exact URL) and how much it will cost, including tax and shipping.

_____

_____

_____

_____

_____

_____

_____

_____

_____

22 Setting Up a Windows Network

Choosing the right networking technologies and hardware is only half of the work—the other half is setting up the network with the needed clients, services, and protocols in Windows. The later versions of Windows (Me, 2000, and XP) make this process simple by including wizards, but a good technician should also know how to do the setup manually. In these projects you will practice both Wizard-based and manual configuration.

> **N O T E**
>
> The projects in this chapter assume that you have the same version of Windows running on two PCs. If you have different versions, use one project's instructions for one of the PCs and another project's instructions for the other.

Project 22A: Creating a Peer-to-Peer Network in Windows 98

Time to Complete: 10 to 20 minutes
Needed: Two PCs running Windows 98; a 10/100BaseT NIC for each PC; an Ethernet hub; Cat5 cable sufficient for connecting each PC to the hub
Reference: Pages 838 through 857 of the textbook

1. Physically configure the network. Do any of the following that are not already done, and place a check mark beside the things you did.

   ❏ Installed the NICs in the PCs.

   ❏ Installed Windows drivers for the NICs so that Windows recognizes them as working properly.

   ❏ Plugged the hub into an AC outlet.

   ❏ Connected the NICs to the hub with Cat5 cable.

2. On each PC, check in Device Manager to make sure the NIC is recognized. If it is not, troubleshoot as needed.

3. On each PC, install the following items from the Network Properties (Control Panel) if any of them are not already installed. Place a check mark next to the ones that you had to install.

   ❏ Adapters: Your NIC should appear on the list of installed network components. If it does not, you did not do step 2 correctly.

   ❏ Clients: Client for Microsoft Networks

   ❏ Services: File and Printer Sharing for Microsoft Networks

   ❏ Protocols: TCP/IP

4. On the Identification tab of the Network Properties box, enter a unique name for each PC in the Computer Name box, enter a common name (the same name for both PCs) in the Workgroup box, and then click OK.

5. If prompted, insert the Windows 98 CD. When the drivers have been installed, you will be prompted to reboot; do so.

6. On each of the PCs, browse the network through Network Neighborhood. If each one cannot see an icon for the other, troubleshoot as needed and then document your steps.

_____

_____

_____

_____

_____

_____

Project 22B: Creating a Peer-to-Peer Network in Windows 2000

Time to Complete: 10 to 20 minutes
Needed: Two PCs running Windows 2000; a 10/100BaseT NIC for each PC; an Ethernet hub; Cat5 cable sufficient for connecting each PC to the hub
Reference: Pages 838 through 857 of the textbook

1. Physically configure the network. Do any of the following that are not already done, and place a check mark beside the things you did.

   ❑ Installed the NICs in the PCs.

   ❑ Installed Windows drivers for the NICs so that Windows recognizes them as working properly.

   ❑ Plugged the hub into an AC outlet.

   ❑ Connected the NICs to the hub with Cat5 cable.

2. On each PC, check in Device Manager to make sure the NIC is recognized. If it is not, troubleshoot as needed.

3. If you installed any drivers on either PC, reboot it to allow Windows to detect your network connection.

4. On the first PC, from the Control Panel, open Network and Dial-Up Connections. If there is already an icon for Local Area Connection, right-click it and check its properties to make sure the following are installed for it. Install any that are missing. Place a check mark next to any that you had to install.

    ❏ Client for Microsoft Networks

    ❏ Internet Protocol (TCP/IP)

    ❏ File and Printer Sharing for Microsoft Networks

    If there is not already an icon for Local Area Connection, double-click Make New Connection and work through the wizard to create it.

5. Repeat step 4 on the other PC.

6. Open My Network Places on each PC and browse to find each other. If the PCs do not see icons for each other, troubleshoot and then document your steps.

    _____

    _____

    _____

    _____

    _____

    _____

Project 22C: Creating a Peer-to-Peer Network in Windows XP

Time to Complete: 10 to 20 minutes

Needed: Two PCs running Windows XP; a 10/100BaseT NIC for each PC; an Ethernet hub; Cat5 cable sufficient for connecting each PC to the hub.

Reference: Pages 838 through 862 of the textbook

1. Physically configure the network. Do any of the following that are not already done, and place a check mark beside the things you did.

    ❏ Installed the NICs in the PCs.

    ❏ Installed Windows drivers for the NICs so that Windows recognizes them as working properly.

    ❏ Plugged the hub into an AC outlet.

    ❏ Connected the NICs to the hub with Cat5 cable.

2. On each PC, check in Device Manager to make sure the NIC is recognized. If it is not, troubleshoot as needed.

3. On each PC, choose Start, point to All Programs, point to Accessories, point to Communications, and then click Network Setup Wizard and work through the wizard to configure the network connectivity. Document any problems or challenges.

_____

_____

_____

_____

_____

_____

4. Open My Network Places on each PC and browse to find each other. If the PCs do not see icons for each other, troubleshoot and then document your steps.

_____

_____

_____

_____

_____

_____

Project 22D: Using Alternative Communications Protocols

Time to Complete: 10 to 20 minutes
Needed: A functioning Ethernet workgroup consisting of two PCs
Reference: Pages 848 through 850 of the textbook

Except for Windows 95, Windows does not install the NetBEUI protocol by default. It can be a very useful protocol for a small home network, however, because it is extremely fast.

1. What network communication protocols are already installed on both of these PCs? Include only the protocols that they currently have in common.

   _____

   _____

2. Install the NetBEUI protocol on both PCs and then remove all other protocols (including TCP/IP).

3. Use Network Neighborhood or My Network Places to confirm that the PCs can see each other on the network. If you have problems, troubleshoot and then document your steps.

   _____

   _____

   _____

   _____

   _____

   _____

   _____

   _____

4. What would be the disadvantage, if any, of running the network like this all the time, without TCP/IP installed?

   _____

   _____

   _____

   _____

5. Reinstall the TCP/IP protocol, so that both PCs have both TCP/IP and NetBEUI installed.

6. Using Windows 98, you can bind certain protocols to certain adapters, so that you could use NetBEUI for your internal network and TCP/IP for your connection to the Internet. Windows 2000 and XP handle this differently; explain how those versions enable you to use certain protocols only for certain connections.

   _____

   _____

   _____

   _____

   _____

   _____

23 Using a Windows Network

Part of the job of a PC technician is to educate end users about features of their hardware and software that they might not be comfortable with on their own. One of these is network usage. End users must know how to share files and printers with one another and how to access the resources that others have made available In these projects you will practice those skills yourself.

Project 23A: Sharing a Folder

Time to Complete: 10 to 20 minutes
Needed: A working peer-to-peer (workgroup) network with two PCs
Reference: Pages 896 through 901 of the textbook

1. Which version of Windows are you using? _____

2. In My Computer, display the contents of the C drive and then create a new folder called *Public*.

3. Share the *Public* folder with Read-Only access. Document the steps you followed. (They will be different depending on the Windows version you are using.)

   _____

   _____

   _____

   _____

   _____

4. After you share the folder, how does its icon look? Draw the icon below.

5. Briefly give an example of a situation in which you would want to share a folder with Read-Only access.

    _____

    _____

    _____

    _____

6. Go to another PC on the network and browse through Network Neighborhood or My Network Places to locate the *Public* folder. If you cannot display it, troubleshoot and then document your steps.

    _____

    _____

    _____

    _____

7. Go back to the first PC and copy a text file into the Public folder.

    ┌─ N O T E ──┐
    │ If you cannot find a text file, create a new one by right-clicking and choosing New and then Text Document. │
    └──┘

8. Go back to the second PC and redisplay the *Public* folder. The new file should be there. If it is not, choose View and then Refresh. If it is still not there, troubleshoot and then document the steps.

    _____

    _____

    _____

    _____

9. From the second PC, try to delete the file in the *Public* folder. What happens?

    _____

10. Go back to the first PC and change the sharing for the *Public* folder so that others have full access to it (not just read-only).

11. Go back to the second PC and try to delete the file. What happens?

    _____

12. Microsoft recommends sharing individual folders rather than entire drives. It especially warns against sharing the C drive in its entirety. What is the possible danger you are being warned about?

_____

_____

_____

_____

Project 23B: Browsing Shared Folders on the Network

Time to Complete: 10 to 20 minutes

Needed: A working peer-to-peer (workgroup) network with two PCs, with at least one folder or drive shared on each PC

Optional: A shared printer

Reference: Pages 889 through 894 of the textbook

1. Open Network Neighborhood (NT, 95, 98) or My Network Places (Me, 2000, XP). List the icons you see at the first level.

_____

_____

_____

_____

2. If icons appear for the individual PCs in the workgroup, go to step 3. If not, browse through the network to find such a list. The exact steps depend on the Windows version you are using. List what you clicked on to get there.

_____

_____

_____

_____

3. Double-click an icon for a PC. The shared drives, folders, and printers on it appear (if any).

   a. Which PC's icon did you click on? _____

   b. What items appeared as shared? _____

4. Click the Back button on the toolbar to go back up one level.

5. On the desktop, create a shortcut to one of the shared drives or folders.

6. Rename the shortcut to a name that will help you remember which computer it came from. What did you name it? _____

7. If you are using Windows Me, 2000, or XP, create a Network Places shortcut to the folder or drive, so that it appears at the top level of the My Network Places folder. List the steps you took to do so.

_____

_____

_____

_____

Project 23C: Sharing a Printer

Time to Complete: 5 to 15 minutes
Needed: A working peer-to-peer (workgroup) network with two PCs; a printer attached directly to one of the PCs; if both PCs are not running the same OS version, you might also need a driver disk for the printer
Reference: Pages 901 through 903 of the textbook

1. On the figure below, label each printer icon with one or more letters as follows.

   Next to the default printer, write *D*.

   Next to each local printer, write *L*.

   Next to each network printer, write *N*.

   Next to each shared local printer, write *S*.

 Epson Stylus COLOR 800 ESC/P 2 on NEWDELL

 Acrobat Distiller 0

 Acrobat PDFWriter 0

 Lexmark Optra S 1855 (MS) 0

 Lexmark Optra S 1855 PS 0

Name: _____

Date: _____

2. On the computer with the printer attached, make sure that the printer's driver is installed correctly and that you can print from it. Troubleshoot as needed and then document your steps.

_____

_____

_____

3. Share the printer with full access for everyone. Document the procedure you followed to do so.

_____

_____

_____

4. Go to the second PC and run the Add Printer Wizard, setting up this printer as a Network printer. If the second PC is running a different OS version, and this printer model is not directly supported in that OS version, you might need a driver disk for the printer. Document your steps here.

_____

_____

_____

_____

_____

_____

5. On the second PC (the one that does *not* have the printer directly attached), open an application, such as a word processor, enter some data, and then try to print it on the shared printer. If you cannot print, troubleshoot and then document your steps.

_____

_____

_____

_____

_____

Name: _____

Date: _____

Project 23D: Mapping a Network Drive

Time to Complete: 4 to 15 minutes
Needed: A PC that is part of a network, with access to at least one shared folder
Reference: Pages 895 through 896 of the textbook

1. What is "mapping a network drive," and why would you want to do it?

   _____
   _____
   _____
   _____
   _____
   _____
   _____
   _____

2. In both the left and right panes below, circle the mapped network drive(s).

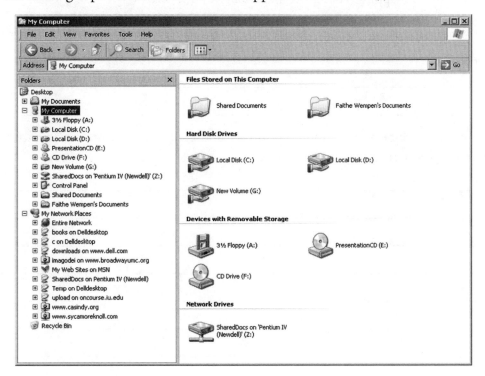

3. Browse the network to find a shared folder to map to a network drive letter.

4. Map that shared folder to an unused drive letter. Document the steps you followed.

   _____

   _____

   _____

   _____

   _____

   _____

   a. What drive letter did you use? _____

   b. Did you set the drive mapping to reconnect automatically each time the PC restarts? _____

5. Open an application, such as a word processing program, and key a few lines in a new file. Save it to the mapped network drive as a new file there. What did you name the file?

   _____

6. Close the application, and open the mapped network drive through My Computer. Find the saved data file you created in step 5, and delete it.

7. Disconnect the drive mapping. Write the steps that you followed.

   _____

   _____

   _____

   _____

8. Drive mapping used to be a much more important and common networking activity than it is today. Explain why it is less popular now than it once was.

   _____

   _____

   _____

   _____

   _____

   _____

   _____

   _____

Project 23E: Exploring Permissions Settings in Windows 2000 or XP

Time to Complete: 10 to 20 minutes
Needed: Two PCs running Windows 2000 or XP, with access to one another in a peer-to-peer workgroup
Reference: Pages 906 through 915 of the textbook

1. This project will refer to the PCs as PC 1 and PC 2. Decide which PC you will designate with which name.

    a. PC 1 is _____

    b. PC 2 is _____

2. On PC 1, create a new folder called *Practice* and share it.

3. On the Sharing tab of the *Practice* folder's Properties dialog box, click the Permissions button. Who has permission to this folder, and what permission do they have?

    _____

    _____

    _____

    _____

4. Close the dialog box without making any changes to the permissions and then close the folder's Properties box.

5. Go to PC 2, start it up, and log in. Make a note of the exact user name you used to log in. If PC 2 is already running, choose Start and then Log Off, and then log in again to ensure you know the exact user name.

6. Go back to PC 1 and then redisplay permissions for the *Practice* folder (step 3). Delete the Everyone group from the list. Add the username who is logged into PC 2 to the Permissions list, and grant that user full access to this folder. Document the steps you followed to add the user and assign the permission.

    _____

    _____

    _____

    _____

    _____

7. Go to PC 2 and try to access the *Practice* folder. If you cannot access it, troubleshoot and then document your steps.

_____

_____

_____

_____

_____

8. On PC 2, log off and then log in as another user. Try to access the *Practice* folder again. Can you access it? _____

9. Go back to PC 1 and add that other user to the permissions for the *Practice* folder. Go back to PC 2 and then try again. Now can you access it? _____

24 Modems

Even though broadband Internet is exploding in popularity, many people still rely on a modem for Internet access. Modems are also employed for other, non-Internet connectivity tasks between computers, such as a user dialing into a private corporate network via a terminal application. These projects provide practice in installing and configuring modems.

Project 24A: Installing an Internal Modem

Time to Complete: 10 to 20 minutes
Needed: A working Windows PC with an available ISA or PCI slot; an ISA or PCI internal modem; Web access
Reference: Pages 939 through 941 of the textbook

1. What safety precautions should you observe when handling and installing an internal modem?

   _____

   _____

   _____

   _____

   _____

2. Describe your modem. Is it PCI or ISA? What is the make and model? Is it Plug-and-Play? What special features does it have, if any? To what standards does it conform? Use the Web to find this information if needed.

   _____

   _____

   _____

   _____

   _____

   _____

   _____

   _____

   If you used the Web, write the URL where you found this information.

   http://_____

3. Download the latest drivers for your modem for your OS version, and store them either on a floppy disk or on a folder on your hard disk that you create for this purpose.

4. In Device Manager, view the list of available IRQs. What IRQs are not currently used by any other device?

   _____

   _____

5. (Non-Plug-and-Play modems only) Set the jumpers on the modem to use one of the available IRQs. If there are also jumpers for setting the I/O address, go back to Device Manager, determine which of the unused I/O addresses the modem will support, and set that jumper as well. Describe what jumper settings you chose.

   _____

   _____

6. Following the safety precautions you listed in step 1, install the modem in any available slot in the PC. Document your steps.

   _____

   _____

   _____

   _____

   _____

   _____

7. Restart the PC, and install the drivers for the modem. The process will be different depending on the modem, the OS version, whether the downloaded drivers were in a Setup utility or a ZIP file, and so on. Describe the process.

   _____

   _____

   _____

   _____

   _____

8. Go to Project 24C, "Testing a Modem."

Name: _____

Date: _____

Project 24B: Installing an External Modem

Time to Complete: 5 to 15 minutes
Needed: A working Windows PC with an available COM port or USB port
(depending on the modem's interface); an external modem
Reference: Pages 942 through 943 of the textbook

1. Describe your modem. Is it serial (COM port) or USB? What is the make and model? Is it Plug-and-Play? What special features does it have, if any? To what standards does it conform? Use the Web to find this information if needed.

   _____

   _____

   _____

   _____

   _____

   _____

   _____

   If you used the Web, write the URL where you found this information.

   http://_____

2. Download the latest drivers for your modem for your OS version, and store them either on a floppy disk or on a folder on your hard disk that you create for this purpose.

3. Connect the modem to an AC outlet.

4. Connect the modem to the PC. If connecting via serial (COM) cable, make sure the PC is off first. If connecting to a USB port, the PC can be either on or off.

5. Restart the PC, and install the drivers for the modem. The process will be different depending on the modem, the OS version, whether the downloaded drivers were in a Setup utility or a ZIP file, and so on. Describe the process.

   _____

   _____

   _____

   _____

   _____

   _____

6. If the PC did not see a Plug-and-Play modem that is attached to a COM port, what would you check?

_____

_____

_____

_____

_____

_____

7. If the PC did not see a Plug-and-Play modem that is attached to a USB port, what would you check?

_____

_____

_____

_____

_____

_____

Project 24C: Testing a Modem

Time to Complete: 5 to 10 minutes
Needed: A working Windows PC with a modem installed (internal or external)
Reference: Pages 943 through 947 of the textbook

1. Ensure that the drivers for the modem are installed. How can you tell?

_____

_____

_____

2. Test the modem by completing the following steps.

   - Windows 95, 98, and Me:

   a. From the Control Panel, double-click Modems.

   b. Click the Diagnostics tab.

   c. Click More Info.

   - Windows 2000 and XP:

   a. From the Control Panel, double-click Phone and Modem Options.

   b. Click the Modems tab.

   c. Double-click the modem you want to check to open its Properties box.

   d. Click the Diagnostics tab and then click Query Modem.

3. Based on the reported results, is the modem working correctly? How can you tell?

   _____

   _____

   _____

4. If the modem is not working correctly, troubleshoot and then document your steps.

   _____

   _____

   _____

   _____

   _____

   _____

5. Connect a telephone line to the Line port on the modem. How can you tell the difference between the Line port and the Phone port?

   _____

   _____

   _____

   _____

6. Connect a telephone to the Phone port on the modem.

7. If there are symbols next to the Phone and Line ports on the modem, rather than words, draw pictures of the symbols.

8. Pick up the telephone receiver and listen for a dial tone. Do you hear one? _____

   If not, troubleshoot and then document your steps.

   _____

   _____

   _____

   _____

Project 24D: Setting Modem Properties in Windows

Time to Complete: 10 to 15 minutes

Needed: A working Windows PC with a modem installed and working (see Project 24C)

Reference: Page 947 of the textbook

1. Open the Properties box for the modem. How did you do it?

   _____

   _____

   _____

2. List at least six properties you can change from the modem's Properties box.

    _____

    _____

    _____

    _____

    _____

    _____

3. What type of Flow Control does your modem use by default?

    _____

4. What type of Error Control does your modem use by default?

    _____

5. Does it use FIFO buffers by default?

    _____

6. What COM port, if any, is assigned to the modem?

    _____

7. What is its maximum speed, as defined from within the Properties box?

    _____

8. Why is the maximum speed in step 7 different from the modem's advertised maximum data transfer rate?

    _____

    _____

    _____

    _____

9. Close the modem's Properties.

Project 24E: Using a Terminal Program

Time to Complete: 10 to 15 minutes
Needed: A working Windows PC with a modem installed and working and HyperTerminal installed
Reference: Pages 956 through 960 of the textbook

1. Start HyperTerminal. After clicking on the Start button, what do you select to open HyperTerminal in your Windows version?

   _____

   _____

2. Set up a new terminal connection that dials your own phone number (just for practice) and save its settings. Name the file anything you like. Write the steps you took to create the new connection.

   _____

   _____

   _____

   _____

   _____

   _____

3. Close any open dialog boxes in HyperTerminal, so you are at the plain white interface screen.

4. Key **ATZ** and then press Enter.

   a. If you do not see what you keyed, what do you need to do in order to see it?

      _____

      _____

   b. If you see double letters of everything you keyed, what do you need to do in order to fix this?

      _____

      _____

5. Do whatever is needed (see step 4) to fix the duplex setting so that one copy of whatever you type appears on-screen.

6. Key **ATZ** again. What does the modem respond with? _____

7. Key the command that turns off the modem speaker. What is that command?

   _____

8. Key the command that turns the speaker back on. What is that command?

   _____

9. Key a command that dials a 1, pauses for two seconds, and then dials your complete phone number, including area code. What is that command?

   _____

10. Key the command that hangs up. What is that command?

    _____

11. Close HyperTerminal.

25 The Internet

The Internet has revolutionized home and business computing, and today nearly every personal computer has some way of accessing it. As a technician you may be supporting a mixture of dial-up and network Internet connections. You might also be called upon to help users configure Web browser software such as Internet Explorer and e-mail software such as Outlook Express. These projects provide an opportunity to practice and demonstrate those skills.

Project 25A: Creating a New Dial-Up Connection

Time to Complete: 10 to 20 minutes
Needed: A working Windows PC with a modem and telephone line access; an account with an ISP
Reference: Pages 950 through 956 of the textbook

1. Which types of Internet connectivity require a Dial-Up Networking (DUN) connection? Circle as many as apply.

   56Kbps modem   Cable   LAN   Two-way satellite

   ISDN   DSL   One-way satellite

2. What information do you need to have available when you create a DUN connection to an ISP? Assume for the moment that you do *not* need to set up any e-mail accounts.

   _____

   _____

   _____

   _____

   _____

3. What Windows version are you using? _____
   a. In your version of Windows, what is the name of the wizard that creates a new DUN connection?

   _____

b. How do you start the wizard beginning from the Windows desktop?

_____

_____

_____

_____

_____

_____

4. Start the wizard you named in step 3, and work through it to create the DUN connection. Document the steps you followed and the information you entered at each step.

_____

_____

_____

_____

_____

_____

_____

5. Use the new DUN connection to connect to the ISP. If the connection will not establish, or will not stay established, troubleshoot and then document your steps.

_____

_____

_____

_____

_____

6. What icon do you see in the notification area when the connection is established? Draw it below.

7. Check your connection by attempting to access the Web. If you cannot get to the Web, troubleshoot and then document your steps.

_____

_____

_____

_____

_____

_____

8. Right-click the icon in the system tray. What options appear on its shortcut menu?

_____

_____

_____

_____

9. Disconnect the DUN connection. How did you do it?

_____

_____

10. Close all open windows. Now assume that you wanted to reestablish your DUN connection. List at least two different ways to do this.

_____

_____

_____

_____

11. If you have two DUN connections, how would Windows know which one is the default or preferred one? Explain how you would set this preference.

_____

_____

_____

_____

_____

_____

_____

_____

Project 25B: Configuring an E-Mail Account

Time to Complete: 5 to 15 minutes

Needed: A Windows PC with Internet access and Outlook Express; the information for setting up a POP or IMAP e-mail account

Reference: Pages 994 through 996 of the textbook

1. Start Outlook Express (OE). What version of OE do you have? How can you tell?

_____

_____

2. Are there currently any e-mail accounts set up in OE? How can you tell?

_____

_____

3. If there are currently e-mail addresses set up, what are the e-mail addresses?

_____

_____

4. Prepare the information you will need to add a POP or IMAP e-mail account to Outlook Express:

E-mail address: _____

Account: _____

Password: _____

Incoming mail server: _____

Outgoing mail server: _____

5. Set up the e-mail account as a new account in Outlook Express. How did you start the Wizard that walks you through this process? What was the name of the Wizard?

_____

_____

6. Test the new e-mail account by sending yourself a message to the same e-mail address. If you do not get a message back, troubleshoot and then document your steps.

_____

_____

_____

_____

_____

_____

7. Label the following items on the Outlook Express screen.

A. Unread message

B. Flagged message

C. Message with an attachment

D. Urgent message

E. Selected message

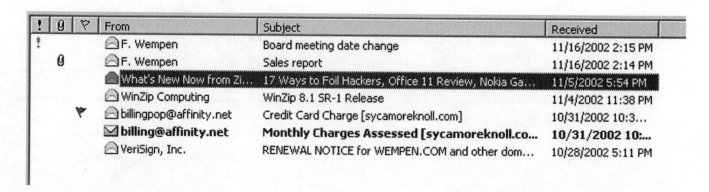

!	0	⚐	From	Subject	Received	
!			F. Wempen	Board meeting date change	11/16/2002 2:15 PM	
	0		F. Wempen	Sales report	11/16/2002 2:14 PM	
			What's New Now from Zi...	17 Ways to Foil Hackers, Office 11 Review, Nokia Ga...	11/5/2002 5:54 PM	
			WinZip Computing	WinZip 8.1 SR-1 Release	11/4/2002 11:38 PM	
		⚐	billingpop@affinity.net	Credit Card Charge [sycamoreknoll.com]	10/31/2002 10:3...	
			billing@affinity.net	**Monthly Charges Assessed [sycamoreknoll.co...**	**10/31/2002 10:...**	
			VeriSign, Inc.	RENEWAL NOTICE for WEMPEN.COM and other dom...	10/28/2002 5:11 PM	

Project 25C: Configuring a Web Browser

Time to Complete: 5 to 15 minutes
Needed: A Windows PC with Internet access and Internet Explorer (IE) 6.0 or higher
Reference: Pages 985 through 989 of the textbook

1. Start Internet Explorer (IE). What version of IE do you have? How can you tell?

   _____

   _____

   _____

   _____

2. What URL is currently set up as the home page?

   http://_____

3. Change the home page to http://www.emcp.com and then describe the steps taken.

   _____

   _____

   _____

   _____

4. Indicate which tab of the Internet Options dialog box you would use to make each change.

   a. Specify the default e-mail application: _____

   b. Choose a default DUN connection: _____

   c. Delete cookies: _____

   d. Block cookies from being received: _____

   e. Block out sexual or violent content: _____

   f. Clear history: _____

   g. Do not play sounds and videos on Web pages _____

   h. Allow downloading of signed ActiveX controls: _____

   i. Turn AutoComplete on and off: _____

   j. Use a proxy server: _____

   k. Make visited hyperlinks a different color: _____

Name: _____

Date: _____

5. Go to http://www.yahoo.com and then change the text size to Largest (from the View menu).

   a. Does at least some of the text change in size immediately? _____

   b. Does some of the text appear not to be affected by this setting? _____

   c. If so, what text is not affected? _____

   d. After you refresh the page (F5), is there any difference? _____

6. Go to http://www.emcp.com/sitemap.php. Then change the text size to Medium (from the View menu).

   a. Does at least some of the text change in size immediately? _____

   b. Does some of the text appear not to be affected by this setting? _____

   c. If so, what text is not affected? _____

   d. Why do you think that some text is affected by the Text Size setting and other text is not?

   _____

   _____

   _____

   _____

7. Make unvisited hyperlinks appear as bright pink (from the tab you indicated in step 4 in the Internet Options box). Then visit the following Web sites and observe whether or not hyperlinks appear pink.

   http://www.msn.com _____

   http://www.yahoo.com _____

   http://www.microsoft.com _____

   http://www.google.com _____

   Why do the hyperlinks on some of these sites not appear pink?

   _____

   _____

   _____

   _____

Project 25D: Configuring Internet Security and Privacy Settings

Time to Complete: 5 to 15 minutes
Needed: A Windows PC with Internet access and Internet Explorer (IE) 6.0 or higher
Reference: Pages 990 through 993 of the textbook

1. What is the difference between security and privacy on the Web? In other words, what does "security" attempt to prevent, and what does "privacy" attempt to prevent?

   _____

   _____

   _____

   _____

2. For each of these scenarios, write an *S* next to the ones that are security activities and a *P* next to the ones that are privacy activities. Some might be both.

   a. Clearing the History list   _____

   b. Preventing cookies from being created on your hard disk   _____

   c. Not allowing passwords to be automatically filled in   _____

   d. Preventing ActiveX controls from running   _____

   e. Preventing scripts from running on Web pages   _____

   f. Blocking cookies from specific Web sites   _____

   g. Using SSL certificates to authenticate the source of Web content _____

   h. Turning off AutoComplete   _____

   i. Emptying the Temporary Internet Files folder   _____

3. Suppose that the owner of your lab PC is concerned that someone will be able to snoop on his computer to find out what Web sites he has been visiting. Completely eradicate all detectable information about the past Web surfing habits on this PC and then document your steps.

_____

_____

_____

_____

_____

_____

_____

_____

_____

4. Is it possible for a computer to get a virus while surfing the Web? If so, explain how this could happen. If not, explain why it is not possible.

_____

_____

_____

_____

_____

5. Set the Security settings on your PC to the highest levels possible. Describe what settings you changed.

_____

_____

_____

6. Spend about 5 minutes visiting popular commercial Web sites. Document any warnings or problems you encountered due to the high security settings.

_____

_____

_____

_____

_____

_____

_____

7. Put the security settings back to their normal values when you are finished with the experiment.

Project 25E: Using a Web Content Filter

Time to Complete: 5 to 15 minutes
Needed: A Windows PC with Internet access and Internet Explorer (IE) 6.0 or higher

---

N O T E

In the Content Advisor, the default advisor is RSACi (Recreational Software Advisory Council Rating Service for the Internet); for this exercise we will be working with the settings for that service. There may be additional filtering services installed on your PC as well.

---

1. In Internet Explorer, enable the Content Advisor.

2. Set all of the RSACi settings to their lowest level (zero), so that no potentially objectionable content will be tolerated.

3. Assign a password to the Content Advisor. What password did you assign?

_____

4. Spend about 5 minutes surfing the Web, intentionally trying to go to some sites that might contain objectionable content. Make notes below documenting each site you tried to visit and what happened.

_____

_____

_____

_____

_____

_____

_____

_____

_____

_____

5. Based on your experiment notes in step 4, what are your conclusions about the usefulness of this filtering software?

_____

_____

_____

_____

_____

_____

PART 6

Understanding and Using Operating Systems

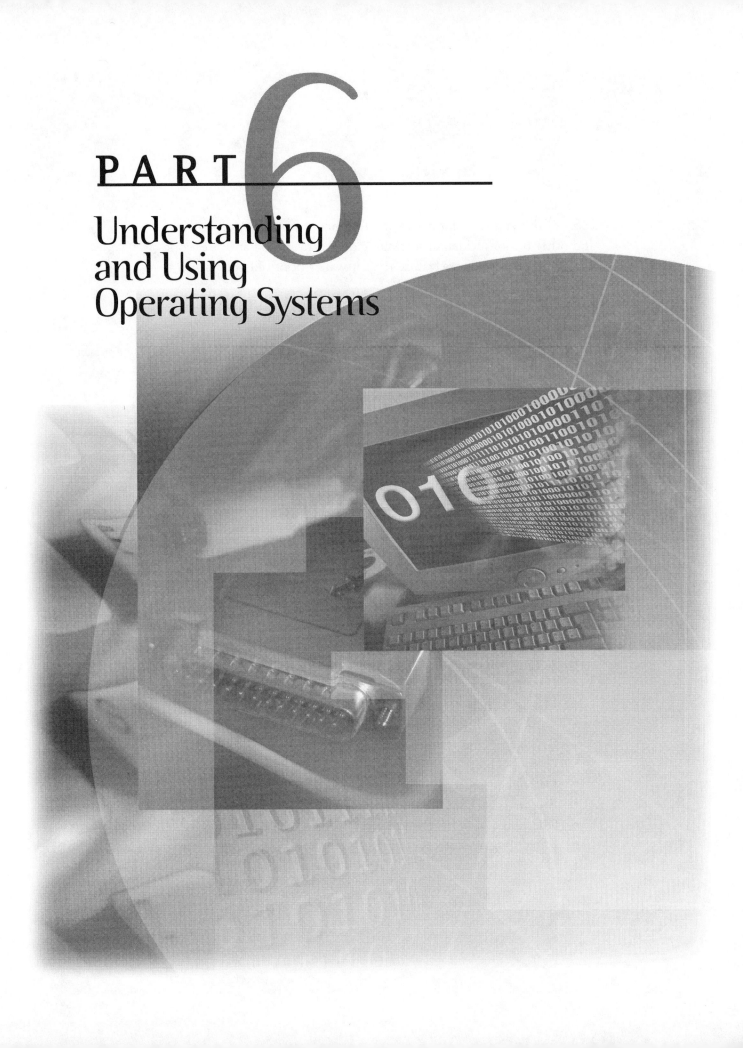

Most of this course so far has focused on hardware and on the drivers and other bits of incidental software required to make hardware work. The next several projects feature the software, specifically operating systems and system utilities.

In this section's projects, you will practice selecting and installing operating systems, starting them up and shutting them down, and troubleshooting their problems and peculiarities. Some of the activities you will demonstrate include:

- Installing Windows from CAB files
- Installing Windows from CD-ROM
- Upgrading the Windows version
- Manually extracting files from CABs
- Setting up dual-boot systems
- Creating a Windows 98 startup disk
- Using alternative boot modes such as Step-by-Step Confirmation and Safe Mode
- Creating an Emergency Repair Disk in Windows 2000
- Repairing a Windows installation
- Using the Windows 2000 Recovery Console
- Editing Autoexec.bat and Config.sys
- Installing and removing applications
- Adding and removing Windows components
- Configuring an MS-DOS program under Windows
- Managing files
- Working with file attributes
- Backing up and restoring files
- Using NTFS file features
- Defragmenting a disk
- Running the Disk Cleanup Wizard
- Checking a disk for errors
- Scheduling a recurring task

26 Selecting and Installing an Operating System

Project 26A: Installing Windows 98 from CABs

Time to Complete: 30 to 60 minutes
Needed: A PC with an empty hard disk; a Windows 98 CD; a CD drive; a Windows 98 startup disk; Web access
Reference: Pages 1052 through 1061 of the textbook

1. (Optional) On the Web, go to the Microsoft Hardware Compatibility List (http://www.microsoft.com/hcl), and check to make sure that all the identifiable hardware on the PC is compatible with Windows 98. Note any potential problems.

   _____

   _____

   _____

   _____

   _____

   If you cannot precisely identify some of the hardware, go to step 2 and sort out any problems later.

2. Boot from the Windows 98 startup disk, and enable CD support.

3. If the hard disk is not already formatted, format it. You might need to partition it first; see Chapter 12 projects for help. Describe what you did.

   _____

   _____

   _____

   _____

   _____

4. From the command prompt, create a new folder called *CABS* on the C drive. What command did you use?

   _____

5. Display a list of the files on the CD with the DIR command. What command did you use for that?

    _____

6. Copy all of the files from the *WIN98* folder on the CD to the *CABS* folder on the hard disk. What command did you use? _____

7. Change to the C:\\ *CABS* folder, key **SETUP**, and then press Enter.

8. Follow the prompts to install Windows 98. Document the steps in the process.

    _____

    _____

    _____

    _____

    _____

    _____

9. Check Device Manager to make sure all installed devices were properly detected. Install drivers for any that were not. Document your steps.

    _____

    _____

    _____

    _____

    _____

    _____

10. If you had to go to any Web sites to get the needed drivers, write the URLs here.

    http:// _____

    http:// _____

    http:// _____

11. If you encountered any problems, write them here, and explain how you solved them.

_____

_____

_____

Project 26B: Installing Windows 2000 from CD-ROM

Time to Complete: 30 to 60 minutes

Needed: A PC with a BIOS capable of booting from CD; an empty hard disk; a CD drive; Windows 2000 CD

Reference: Pages 1062 through 1065 of the textbook

1. (Optional) On the Web, go to the Microsoft Hardware Compatibility List (http://www.microsoft.com/hcl), and check to make sure that all the identifiable hardware on the PC is compatible with Windows 2000. Note any potential problems.

_____

_____

_____

_____

_____

If you cannot precisely identify some of the hardware, go to step 2 and sort out any problems later.

2. Set up the PC's BIOS to boot first from the CD. Document the steps you took to do this.

_____

_____

_____

_____

3. Boot from the CD, and work through the on-screen instructions to start Windows 2000 Setup.

4. When prompted about partitions and formatting, delete all existing partitions and create a single new partition. Format it with the NTFS file system. Document the steps you took.

_____

_____

_____

_____

_____

_____

5. Continue the Windows 2000 Setup process to completely install Windows 2000. Document the steps you took.

_____

_____

_____

_____

6. Check Device Manager to make sure all installed devices were properly detected. Install drivers for any that were not. Document your steps.

_____

_____

_____

_____

_____

_____

_____

7. If you had to go to any Web sites to get the needed drivers, write the URLs here.

   http:// _____

   http:// _____

   http:// _____

8. If you encountered any problems, write them here and explain how you solved them.

   _____

   _____

   _____

Project 26C: Upgrading from Windows 98 to Windows 2000

Time to Complete: 30 to 60 minutes
Needed: A PC with Windows 98 installed and a CD drive; a Windows 2000 Setup CD; Web access
Reference: Pages 1055, 1062 through 1065 of the textbook

1 From Device Manager, print a report that lists the installed hardware.

2. Go to the Hardware Compatibility List on the Web (http://www.microsoft.com/hcl), and check to make sure all your hardware is supported. List any potential incompatibilities.

   _____

   _____

   _____

   _____

   _____

   _____

3. Decide what to do with any incompatible or unlisted devices. You can remove them to avoid potential problems, or you can try upgrading Windows anyway and deal with problems later if they occur. List your decisions about each of the devices from step 2.

_____

_____

_____

_____

_____

4. Create a new folder on the hard disk called *Win2000Drivers*. Download the Windows 2000 drivers for all essential components from their respective manufacturers' Web sites. List the devices and their URLs.

_____

_____

_____

_____

_____

5. With Windows 98 running, insert the Windows 2000 Setup CD. The Setup program should start automatically. If it does not, what is wrong and how can you fix it?

_____

_____

_____

6. Follow the prompts to upgrade to Windows 2000. Document the steps.

_____

_____

_____

_____

_____

_____

_____

7. Check Device Manager to make sure all installed devices were properly detected. Install drivers for any that were not. Document your steps.

_____

_____

_____

_____

_____

_____

_____

_____

8. Indicate any problems you encountered and explain how you solved them.

_____

_____

_____

Project 26D: Manually Extracting a File from a CAB

Time to Complete: 5 to 10 minutes
Needed: A PC with Windows 98 installed; the Setup CD for the same version; a Windows 98 startup floppy
Reference: Pages 1068 through 1070 of the textbook

CAUTION

This project deals with HIMEM.SYS, an extremely important file. Windows will not work without it. Therefore, make sure that the version of Windows installed on your PC is the same as the version on the Setup CD that you have, and also the same version as on the startup floppy.

Suppose you have a startup error message saying that HIMEM.SYS is corrupt. You need to extract a new copy of it from the Windows 98 CD. As a reminder, here is the syntax for the EXTRACT command.

EXTRACT [/Y] [/A] [/D | /E] [/L dir] cabinetfile [filename]

/Y	Does not prompt before overwriting an existing copy.
/A	Searches all CAB files in the specified location, starting with the one specified by the *cabinetfile* variable.
/D	Displays the cabinet directory. If you use this switch along with using a file name, it will only display the list and will not extract anything.
/E	Extract all. You can use this instead of *.* for the name to extract all files.
/L dir	Location to place the extracted files. The default is the current directory.
cabinetfile	The name of the cabinet file, either the only one or the one to start with depending on whether you have used the /A switch.
filename	The name of the file you want to extract. You can use multiple files separated by spaces, or you can use wildcards * or ?. This is optional; if you leave it out it will extract all the files in the specified cabinet file.

1. Start the PC using the Windows 98 startup disk. Enable CD support when prompted.

2. Rename the HIMEM.SYS file in the C:*Windows* folder HIMEM.BAK. What command did you key?

   _____

3. Make a new directory called RECOVER on the C drive. What command did you key?

   _____

4. Extract the file HIMEM.SYS from one of the cabinet files on the CD to the C:*RECOVER* folder. Assuming that you do not know exactly which cab file contains HIMEM.SYS, what command syntax will you use?

   _____

5. Copy C:\RECOVER\HIMEM.SYS to C:\WINDOWS\HIMEM.SYS.

6. Restart Windows normally.

Project 26E: Setting up a Dual-Booting System with Windows 98 and Windows 2000

Time to Complete: 60 to 90 minutes
Needed: A PC with an empty hard disk (or one containing nothing you need to keep); a Windows 98 startup floppy; a Windows 98 Setup CD; a Windows 2000 Setup CD
Reference: Pages 1056 through 1057, 1066 of the textbook

1. If you have a single physical hard disk, how many logical drives must you create in order to dual-boot between two different operating systems?

   _____

2. If you want to dual-boot between Windows 98 and Windows 2000, which should you install first and why?

   _____

   _____

   _____

3. Boot the PC with the Windows 98 startup floppy, and enable CD support.

4. Delete all the existing partitions on the drive. What utility are you using to work with the partitions?

    _____

5. Create a primary and an extended partition, and create a single logical drive on each.

6. Reboot and then format the C drive with the FORMAT command. Which file system did it use: FAT16 or FAT32? How do you know?

    _____

    _____

    _____

7. Install Windows 98 on the C drive. Document any problems you encountered and what you did to fix them.

    _____

    _____

    _____

    _____

    _____

    _____

    _____

8. After Windows 98 is completely installed, set up the BIOS Setup to boot first from the CD.

9. Boot from the Windows 2000 CD, and install Windows 2000 on the logical drive on the extended partition. Allow the Setup program to format the drive with the NTFS file system.

10. After Windows 2000 is completely installed, reboot. A Startup menu appears so you can choose which OS to boot into. What is the exact wording of the names of the OSes on this menu?

    _____

    _____

11. How many seconds does it wait for your response before booting into the default OS?

    _____

12. Which one is the default OS?

    _____

13. Describe how you would make the other OS the default.

_____

_____

_____

_____

_____

27 The Boot Process

"It won't start" is a very common customer complaint, and there can be many different reasons behind this complaint. A successful PC technician needs a standard troubleshooting procedure for startup problems, but also needs to know when to deviate from it and try something else. In these projects you will get a chance to experiment with many different Windows startup options and special modes to get a feel for what is available when you run into real-world problems.

Project 27A: Creating a Windows 98 Startup Disk

Time to Complete: 10 to 20 minutes
Needed: A PC with Windows 98 installed; the Windows 98 Setup CD; a blank floppy disk (or one containing files you do not wish to keep)
Reference: Pages 1106 through 1109 of the textbook

N O T E

This project can also be done with Windows 95 or Windows Me, if Windows 98 is not available.

---

1. Describe a situation in which it would be useful to have a Windows startup disk.

   _____

   _____

   _____

   _____

   _____

2. What is the main difference between a Windows 95 startup disk and one for Windows 98?

   _____

   _____

   _____

3. From the Control Panel, open Add/Remove Programs and go to the Startup Disk tab.

4. Insert a floppy disk and then click Create Disk. Then follow the prompts to create a bootable startup disk.

   a. Did the Create Disk utility prompt you for the Windows CD? _____

   b. Approximately how long did the process take (in seconds)? _____

5. List six files on the startup floppy that have the extension .SYS.

    _____

    _____

    _____

6. Why are there so many different CD-ROM drivers on the startup floppy?

    _____

    _____

    _____

7. Why does the FORMAT command not appear when you list the contents of the startup floppy at a command prompt or within a Windows file management window?

    _____

    _____

    _____

    _____

8. Boot from the startup floppy disk to test it, and enable CD support when prompted. Time the boot process with a clock that has a seconds counter.

    a. How long (in seconds) did the boot process take? _____

    b. When it is finished booting, test it by displaying a list of the files on a data CD (with the DIR command). How many megabytes of data are on the CD? _____

9. Reboot from the startup floppy again, and this time do not enable CD support. Time the boot process again.

    a. How long (in seconds) did the boot process take? _____

    b. Is the CD drive accessible after this boot? _____

Name: _____

Date: _____

Project 27B: Booting Windows 98 Using Step-by-Step Confirmation

Time to Complete: 5 minutes
Needed: A PC with Windows 98 installed
Reference: Page 1094 of the textbook

1. Describe a situation in which Step-by-Step Confirmation when booting would be useful.

    _____

    _____

    _____

    _____

    _____

2. Display the Windows 98 Startup menu as the PC is starting up.

    a. What key do you press? _____

    b. When do you press it?

    _____

    c. How can you tell if you did not press it quickly enough and need to reboot and try again?

    _____

3. Restart the PC and, as it is booting, press the key you indicated in step 2 (at the proper time, which you also indicated in step 2) to display the Windows 98 Startup menu. From there, select Step-by-Step Confirmation.

4. At each of the yes/no questions that appears, key **Y**. List at least six items that the process asks you to confirm.

    _____

    _____

    _____

    _____

    _____

    _____

Chapter 27

Project 27C: Booting Windows 2000 in Safe Mode

Time to Complete: 5 to 15 minutes
Needed: A PC with Windows 2000 installed
Reference: Pages 1097 through 1100 of the textbook

1. Describe a situation in which Safe Mode when booting would be useful.

   _____

   _____

   _____

   _____

   _____

2. What types of drives are not accessible in Safe Mode?

   _____

   _____

   _____

3. List three reasons why you would not want to run your PC in Safe Mode all of the time.

   _____

   _____

   _____

4. Start up Windows 2000, and boot to the Windows 2000 Advanced Options menu. Explain how you did that.

   _____

   _____

   _____

5. Choose Safe Mode from the Advanced Options menu, and allow the computer to continue booting.

6. When Windows is finished booting, restart it, and this time choose Safe Mode with Command Prompt. Describe a situation in which Safe Mode with Command Prompt would be useful.

_____

_____

_____

_____

_____

_____

7. Restart again, and this time boot normally.

Project 27D: Creating a Windows 2000 Emergency Repair Disk (ERD)

Time to Complete: 5 to 10 minutes
Needed: A PC with Windows 2000 installed
Reference: Pages 1109 through 1110 of the textbook

1. Answer the following questions about Windows 2000 ERDs.

a. Are they bootable? _____

b. Do they contain Windows startup files? _____

c. Do they contain repair utility applications? _____

d. Why would having one be useful? _____

_____

_____

_____

e. What Windows utility do you use to create one?

_____

_____

f. If you ever needed to use your ERD to repair Windows, what CD or utility would you need to have?

_____

_____

2. Create an ERD. Document your steps.

_____

_____

_____

_____

_____

3. See Project 27E to use the ERD as part of the Windows 2000 repair process.

Project 27E: Repairing a Windows 2000 Installation

Time to Complete: 10 to 15 minutes
Needed: A PC with Windows 2000 installed
Optional: An ERD for this PC (from Project 27D)
Reference: Page 1110 of the textbook

1. Describe a situation in which repairing a Windows 2000 installation would be useful, as opposed to completely reinstalling Windows.

_____

_____

_____

_____

2. What role does an ERD play in the repair process?

_____

_____

_____

3. Set up the PC's BIOS to boot first from the CD drive.

4. Boot from the Windows 2000 Setup CD and allow the Windows Setup process to begin.

5. At the Welcome to Setup screen, key **R** to choose the Repair option, and then key **R** again to choose the Emergency Repair Process.

6. When asked to choose between Manual and Fast repair, key **F** to choose Fast.

7. When prompted, insert your ERD and then press Enter. (If you do not have an ERD, when prompted for it press *L* and follow the prompts.)

8. Finish working through the repair process by following the on-screen prompts.

Project 27F: Using the Windows 2000 Recovery Console

Time to Complete: 10 to 15 minutes
Needed: A PC with Windows 2000 installed; a Windows 2000 Setup CD
Reference: Pages 1110 through 1112 of the textbook

1. Describe a situation in which using the Windows 2000 Recovery Console would be useful, rather than using the Repair process from Project 27E.

_____

_____

_____

_____

_____

2. Set up the PC's BIOS to boot first from the CD drive.

3. Boot from the Windows 2000 Setup CD and allow the Windows Setup process to begin.

4. At the Welcome to Setup screen, key **R** to choose the Repair option, and then key **C** to choose the Recovery Console.

5. Key **1** and then press Enter to select the first Windows 2000 installation.

6. Key the administrator password for this PC and then press Enter.

7. Use the CD and DIR commands to explore the hard disk from the command prompt. If you encounter any folders you cannot access, or any behavior that differs from a normal command prompt from within Windows, list these problems here.

_____

_____

_____

_____

_____

_____

8. When the results of a command require more than one screen to display:

   a. What key can you press to scroll the display one *page* at a time? _____

   b. What key can you press to scroll the display one *line* at a time? _____

9. Key **HELP** and then press Enter. What happens?

_____

_____

_____

10. What is the difference between FIXBOOT and FIXMBR? Use the information provided by the HELP system if you do not already know.

_____

_____

_____

_____

_____

_____

11. What does DISKPART do?

_____

12. What does EXIT do?

_____

13. Exit from the Recovery Console and reboot normally.

Project 27G: Editing AUTOEXEC.BAT and CONFIG.SYS

Time to Complete: 10 to 15 minutes
Needed: A PC running Windows 98; the startup floppy you created in
Project 27A; another floppy disk (blank)
Reference: Pages 1083 through 1087 of the textbook

1. In Notepad, open the file CONFIG.SYS from the startup floppy and then answer the following questions about its contents.

    a. What is the purpose of the words in square brackets, such as [menu]?

    _____

    b. What does Device= do when it precedes the name of a driver?

    _____

    c. What is the purpose of the switch /D:mscd001 that follows some of the CD drivers?

    _____

2. In Notepad, open the file AUTOEXEC.BAT from the startup floppy and then answer the following questions about its contents.

    a. What is the purpose of the ECHO OFF command?

    _____

    b. What is the purpose of the @ sign that precedes the ECHO OFF command?

    _____

    c. What is the purpose of the CLS command?

    _____

    d. What is the purpose of the Echo command when text follows it, such as *Echo Your computer will now restart.*

    _____

    e. What is the purpose of the Prompt command?

    _____

3. In the AUTOEXEC.BAT file, find the following line.

   `echo The diagnostic tools were successfully loaded to drive %RAMD%.`

   Directly below that line, add the following line.

   pause

   Save the file and then exit Notepad.

4. Restart the PC, and boot from the floppy. Do not load CD support. What has changed about the startup process because of the line you added in step 3?

   _____

   _____

   _____

5. Restart Windows, and reopen the file AUTOEXEC.BAT from the floppy disk in Notepad. Notice that this is not just a simple list of commands; the logical flow branches off depending on various conditions. For example, notice the :ERROR, :EXT, and :QUIT sections (each section name preceded by a colon) and the references to those sections in lines beginning with IF, such as IF "%config%"=="NOCD" GOTO QUIT. On the next page, draw a flow chart that illustrates the logical flow of the commands in the AUTOEXEC.BAT file.

Flow chart for step 5:

28 Working with Applications

End users can install their own applications in most cases, but when something goes wrong, a PC technician may need to step in and help correct the problem. In these projects you will perform a routine installation and removal of an application, install and remove some Windows components, and then look at some issues involved in installing and running MS-DOS applications under Windows.

Project 28A: Installing an Application

Time to Complete: 5 to 20 minutes
Needed: A Windows PC; a Windows-based application on CD that has not yet been installed on this PC
Reference: Pages 1124 through 1130 of the textbook

1. What application are you installing? _____

2. What version number is it? _____

3. Insert the CD into the drive.

   a. Does the Setup program start automatically? _____

   b. If the Setup program did not start automatically, how could you start the Setup utility?

   _____

4. Install the application. Document your steps.

   _____

   _____

   _____

   _____

   _____

   _____

   _____

   _____

5. What is the URL for the application's Web site?

   http://_____

6. Go to the Web site in step 5 and download and install any patches or updates that are available. Describe what you downloaded and installed.

_____

_____

_____

7. Run the application. If you have any problems, troubleshoot using what you know of Windows applications and using any troubleshooting information you can find at the application's Web site. Describe the troubleshooting process and results.

_____

_____

_____

_____

_____

_____

_____

_____

_____

_____

Project 28B: Removing an Application

Time to Complete: 5 minutes
Needed: A Windows PC with at least one application installed
Reference: Pages 1132 through 1136 of the textbook

For this exercise, you will be removing the application you installed in Project 28A. If you did not do Project 28A, uninstall any unneeded application.

1. Rank the following in order of preference for uninstalling.

_____ Uninstall utility on the Start menu, in the same submenu as the application itself

_____ Add/Remove Programs removal

_____ Delete the program files manually

2. Locate the application on the Start menu. Does there appear to be an Uninstall utility associated with it?
_____

3. Open Add/Remove Programs in the Control Panel, and locate the application on the list of installed applications.

4. Is there a single Change/Remove button for this application, or are there separate Change and Remove buttons? Circle the button set below that most resembles your application's buttons.

| Change/Remove | | Change | Remove |

5. Remove the application, and document the steps.

_____

_____

_____

_____

_____

_____

6. Did the removal utility prompt you to restart your PC at the end? _____

7. Restart if prompted.

Project 28C: Adding and Removing Windows Components

Time to Complete: 5 minutes to 10 minutes
Needed: A Windows PC; the Setup CD for the installed version of Windows
Reference: Pages 1137 through 1140 of the textbook

1. From the Control Panel, open Add/Remove Programs and display the Add/Remove Windows Components pane.

2. What Windows version are you using? _____

   Give the top level categories in the Add/Remove Windows Components list in your Windows version.

   _____

   _____

   _____

   _____

   _____

   _____

   _____

3. Choose a component that is not currently installed, and install it. List your steps, including the name of the component you chose.

   _____

   _____

   _____

   _____

   _____

   _____

4. Remove the component you just installed.

5. Suppose you want to set up a PC so that the Windows CD will never be required when adding Windows components. Describe how you would do this.

   _____

   _____

   _____

   _____

   _____

   _____

Project 28D: Installing and Running an MS-DOS Program

Time to Complete: 10 to 20 minutes
Needed: A Windows PC; Web access
Reference: Pages 1140 through 1150 of the textbook

1. Visit a Web site that contains shareware, and find and download an MS-DOS–based application. Create a new folder on your hard disk called *Downloads*, and store the downloaded file there.

   a. What Web site did you visit to find shareware?

   _____

   b. What application did you choose to download?

   _____

2. Do what is necessary to install the downloaded software. Some of the things you might need to do could include the following.

   • **Downloading and installing an unzipping program** such as WinZip (www.winzip.com), if the downloaded file is a ZIP file and you do not have an unzip utility. Windows XP has unzipping capability built-in; other Windows versions do not.

   • **Unzipping a compressed archive (ZIP) file.** Most MS-DOS programs are distributed in this format, whereas most Windows programs are distributed as executable (EXE) installer programs. If you unzip, place the unzipped files in your *Downloads* folder.

   • **Running a Setup utility.** You might want to do this from a command prompt rather than from within Windows. If the Setup program wants to make changes to your startup files, do not let it.

   Describe what you had to do in order to install the software.

   _____

   _____

   _____

   _____

   _____

3. Try running the DOS application, either from a command prompt or by double-clicking its icon in a file management window. When you are finished, return to Windows.

4. If the application appeared to work without problems, create a shortcut for it on the desktop. If it does not work, what is the problem? After describing it, see Project 28E to troubleshoot.

_____

_____

_____

_____

_____

Project 28E: Configuring an MS-DOS Program

Time to Complete: 10 to 20 minutes
Needed: A Windows PC; Web access
Reference: Pages 1144 through 1149 of the textbook

1. Setting the properties for an MS-DOS program creates a shortcut to it; this is its PIF file (although in later Windows versions it does not have a PIF extension). In the following figure, circle the shortcut that has been created.

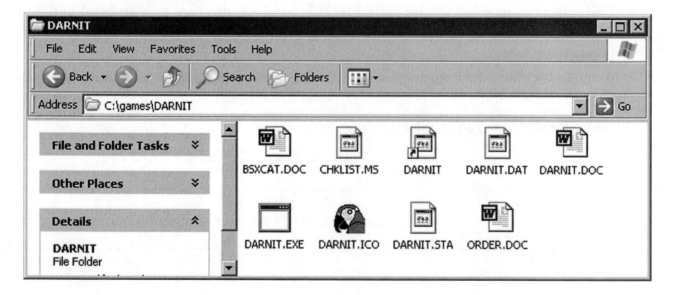

2. Do project 28D if you have not done it already so you have an MS-DOS application installed on your PC. It does not necessarily need to be working very well at this point.

3. Right-click the executable file for the application and choose Properties. Then adjust the properties to correct the problem(s) you are experiencing with the application, if any. Explain what you did and why.

_____

_____

_____

_____

_____

_____

4. Did the above fix the problem? If not, did the symptoms change at all? Explain.

_____

_____

_____

_____

5. (Optional) If you have Windows XP, and the MS-DOS application is still not working correctly, try running the MS-DOS Compatibility Wizard to set up the application to run as a different Windows version. Try several versions. Describe your results.

_____

_____

_____

_____

_____

_____

29 Managing Files

Managing files is an everyday part of most computer users' lives. You probably already know how to move and copy files from place to place, as well as how to rename and delete them. But if you are not as comfortable as you want to be with those activities, or if you are not completely familiar with Microsoft Backup or NTFS features, these projects will help you brush up on your skills.

Project 29A: Selecting Files

Time to Complete: 5 minutes
Needed: A PC with Windows installed
Reference: Page 1171 of the textbook

1. Open My Computer and then open the C drive.

2. View the files in List view. How did you change to List view?

    _____

3. Select all the files and folders on the C drive. There are several ways to do this; which method did you use?

    _____

4. Deselect the selected files. How did you do this? _____

5. Select three different folders that are not near each other. What key did you hold down as you clicked on each file? _____

6. List four different actions you could perform on the selected files as a group.

    _____

    _____

    _____

    _____

Project 29B: File Management Practice

Time to Complete: 10 to 15 minutes
Needed: A PC with Windows installed; a blank floppy disk
Reference: Pages 1167 through 1171 of the textbook

1. Given that when you install a Windows application, it automatically creates a new folder for itself, why would an end user ever need to create a folder manually? Give at least two examples.

    _____

    _____

    _____

    _____

    _____

2. List at least three areas within Windows where you can copy, rename, and delete files.

    _____

    _____

    _____

3. Using the Search (or Find) feature in Windows, find all the files on your hard disk that have a .TXT extension.

4. Copy all of these files to a blank floppy disk.

5. Rename each of the copied text files on the floppy disk with names beginning with the letter *A*. (Use any names you want.)

6. Create a new folder on the C drive called *A-FILES* and move all the text files from the floppy disk into it.

7. Delete two of the text files in the C:*A-FILES* folder.

8. Open a command prompt window. Do the remaining steps at the command prompt, and for each step write the exact command you used.

9. Rename all the files in the C:*A-FILES* folder so that they begin with the letter *B*. _____

10. Rename the *A-FILES* folder to *B-FILES*. _____

11. Make a copy of one of the text files and name the copy with a name that begins with the letter *C*.

    _____

12. Move all the files that begin with *B* to the floppy disk. _____

13. Delete all remaining files from the C:*B-FILES* folder. _____

14. Create a new folder within the *B-FILES* folder called *Extra*. _____

15. Copy all the files from the floppy disk to the *Extra* folder. _____

16. If you wanted to delete the *B-FILES* folder, what steps would you need to take?

_____

_____

_____

_____

_____

_____

17. Delete the *B-FILES* folder, following the procedure you outlined in step 16.

Project 29C: Working with File Attributes

Time to Complete: 5 to 15 minutes
Needed: A PC with Windows installed
Reference: Pages 1174 through 1176 of the textbook

Complete Project 29B before this project; you will need the floppy disk from that project that contains text files.

1. Using Windows Explorer, create a new folder called *Practice* on the C drive.

2. In Windows, set the properties for the *Practice* folder to Read Only. Describe how you did this.

_____

3. Which of the following are you able to do to the *Practice* folder while it is set to Read Only? Try each one, and write *N* next to the ones you are not able to do and *Y* next to the ones you can do.

_____ a. Copy a file into it

_____ b. Move the folder to the C:\Windows folder

_____ c. Delete the folder

_____ d. Rename the folder

_____ e. Copy the folder to a floppy disk

4. Open a command prompt window, and remove the Read-Only attribute from the *Practice* folder using a command-line command. Write the command you used.

_____

Name: _____

Date: _____

5. Using the command prompt, turn on the Read Only attribute for all the files on the floppy disk.

6. Copy the files from the floppy disk to the C:*Practice* folder.

7. From Windows Explorer, check the properties for the files in the C:*Practice* folder. Did the attributes get copied when you copied the files? _____

8. From Windows Explorer, select all the files in the C:*Practice* folder, and remove the Read Only attribute from all of the files at once.

Project 29D: Backing Up and Restoring Files

Time to Complete: 5 to 15 minutes
Needed: A PC with Windows 2000 Professional or XP Professional Edition and the Backup utility installed
Reference: Pages 1182 through 1184 of the textbook

┌─ N O T E ───
You cannot use Windows XP Home Edition for this exercise because it does not include the Backup utility.
└──

1. Name at least two advantages of using Microsoft Backup instead of copying files manually to a removable disk.

_____

_____

_____

_____

2. Name at least two advantages of copying files manually to a removable disk instead of using Microsoft Backup.

_____

_____

_____

_____

3. List at least three types of disks to which Microsoft Backup will back up data.

_____

_____

_____

_____

4. Start the Backup utility, and back up at least three data files from the *My Documents* folder to a floppy disk. Or, if you do not have any files there, back up any three other files from the C drive.

> ┌─ **N O T E** ──
> │ The *My Documents* folder is located on the same drive as Windows, in the *Documents and Settings*\username folder.
> └──

5. Save the list of files you backed up as a backup set named Practice, and exit the Backup utility.
6. Reopen the Backup utility, and restore the backed-up files.

Project 29E: Using NTFS File Features

Time to Complete: 5 to 15 minutes
Needed: A PC with a hard disk that uses the NTFS file system; a floppy disk
Reference: Pages 1176 through 1181 of the textbook

1. Create a new folder on the NTFS hard disk called *Compress*.

2. Turn on NTFS compression for the *Compress* folder. Explain how you did it.

_____

_____

_____

3. Copy two files into the *Compress* folder and then check those files' NTFS attributes. Do the file

attributes show that they are compressed? _____

4. Copy the files to the floppy disk.

   a. Are they still compressed? _____

   b. How do you know?

_____

_____

5. Uncompress the *Compress* folder.

6. Rename the *Compress* folder to *Encrypt*.

7. Turn on NTFS encryption for the *Encrypt* folder.

8. Are the files in the *Encrypt* folder encrypted? How do you know?

   _____

   _____

9. Copy the files from the *Encrypt* folder to the floppy disk.

   a. Are they still encrypted? _____

   b. How do you know?

   _____

   _____

10. Log off Windows, and log in as a different user.

11. Attempt to access the *Encrypt* folder. What happens?

   _____

12. Attempt to remove the encryption from the *Encrypt* folder. What happens?

   _____

13. Log off Windows, and log back in as the original user.

14. Remove the encryption from the *Encrypt* folder.

30 Optimizing and Troubleshooting Windows

Windows comes with a variety of useful utilities for optimizing Windows performance and fixing problems with the file system and the Registry. In these projects you will get some hands-on practice with several of these utilities.

Project 30A: Defragmenting a Disk

Time to Complete: 10 to 60 minutes depending on disk size and amount of fragmentation
Needed: A PC with Windows installed
Reference: Pages 1209 through 1212 of the textbook

1. What does defragmenting do, and why is it advantageous to do it?

   _____

   _____

   _____

   _____

   _____

   _____

2. Start the Disk Defragmenter, and check the amount of fragmentation on the disk.

   a. What is the percentage of fragmented files? _____

   b. What steps did you take to find out the amount of fragmentation?

   _____

   _____

   _____

   _____

3. Defragment the disk. How long did it take? _____

Project 30B: Running the Disk Cleanup Wizard

Time to Complete: 5 minutes
Needed: A PC with a version of Windows installed that includes the Disk Cleanup Wizard
Reference: Pages 1212 through 1213 of the textbook

1. Which versions of Windows have the Disk Cleanup Wizard?

   _____

2. Start the Disk Cleanup Wizard. Explain how you did it.

   _____

3. Examine the details of the recommendation. What categories of items does it suggest, and how many kilobytes can be saved in each category?

   _____

   _____

   _____

   _____

   _____

4. Follow the recommendations and then clean up the disk.

5. Repeat the process for each hard drive on your system if you have more than one.

Project 30C: Checking a Disk for Errors

Time to Complete: 5 minutes to several hours, depending on the size of the disk and the settings chosen
Needed: A PC with a version of Windows installed
Reference: Pages 1225 through 1230 of the textbook

1. What version of Windows do you have? _____

2. What is the name of the utility in this Windows version that checks a disk for errors?

   _____

3. Start the utility. List the steps you followed to do so.

_____

_____

4. If you want the utility to automatically fix any errors it finds, what option do you turn on?

_____

5. If you want the utility to check the disk physically sector-by-sector as well as perform a logical check, what option do you turn on?

_____

6. Check the disk for logical errors only.

   a. How long did the check take? _____

   b. Did it restart during the process? If so, how many times? _____

   c. Were any errors found? If so, what were they?

   _____

   _____

   _____

7. Check the disk for both physical and logical errors, automatically correcting any errors found.

Project 30D: Scheduling a Recurring Task

Time to Complete: 5 to 10 minutes

Needed: A PC with a version of Windows installed that includes the Task Scheduler

Reference: Pages 1231 through 1232 of the textbook

1. Which versions of Windows do NOT include the Task Scheduler?

_____

2. Some versions of Windows have a Maintenance Wizard that enables you to configure a few select utilities as scheduled tasks.

   a. Does your version have this?_____

   b. If your version of Windows has this, run it, and set up each utility to run once a month, on a day and time of your choice.

c. What were the utilities and what dates and times did you choose for each?

_____

_____

_____

_____

3. Open the Scheduled Tasks window, and start the Scheduled Task Wizard. How did you do this?

_____

4. Schedule the Windows Update utility to run at midnight on the first day of every month. Or, if Windows Update is not available on the list of applications, set up any other application to run then. Describe your steps.

_____

_____

_____

_____

_____

_____

_____